PORTLAND

Happy Hour
GUIDEBOOK

2010 EDITION

Portland Happy Hour Guidebook

Fourth Edition
Copyright ©2009-2010 Half-Full Enterprises

ISBN: 978-0-9791201-8-3

All research, reviews, illustrations, maps and design
by Cindy Anderson

Cover art by Amanda Bodack

Printing by Oregon Lithoprint; McMinnville, OR

Half-Full Enterprises

10350 N. Vancouver Way; Suite 173; Portland, OR 97217
www.happyhourguidebook.com
email: pdxinfo@happyhourguidebook.com

How to use this book

Portland is a HAPPY city! But given the plethora of Happy Hour choices in town and around, it can be hard to figure out where to go. In an effort to make things easier, and help lead you to that perfect place for the occasion, this book lists Happy Hours based on "mood." Feeling spicy? Craving a steak? Girls' night out for cocktails? You'll find just what you need instantly. The **alphabetical index** is in the back, with the **mood listings** located in front. **Maps** will guide you by area.

The ratings within follow a very objective and consistent checklist and formula.* All Happy Hours are *not* created equal! But pretty much every Happy Hour is fun, so pick one, or two, and enjoy!

* *See pages 30–33.*

Factoids & Tipsys

- Lots of places **go all night** ('til close) on Sunday or on another weeknight. Look for the ★s in this book to most easily find extended hours.

- **Happy Hour ENDING times** are listed on the website via the MAPS tab. View these maps on your **iPhone!** Refer to the restaurant's rating page in book for full information, ratings & exact hours.

- Be aware of the Happy Hour **end-time** and pad your order by at least 10 minutes. Ask your waiter.

- Incorporate another **activity** such as a movie, a concert, or a long walk into your night out.

- Not all places can accommodate larger **groups.** Call first. It's fun to organize a get-together!

- Sign up for the **email** list at your favorite restaurants. You'll be in the know about special events and offers. And maybe get a coupon here and there too.

- Live in gratitude—most cities do not have Happy Hours. I know—shocking! And we have the *best.*

- Things change! Please **report changes** you find to: pdxinfo@happyhourguidebook.com. Also, sign up for the monthly newsletter to be in-the-know.

- Check in with the **website** to keep up with changes!

www.happyhourguidebook.com

Contents

(You'll need to reference this a lot)

Key

AL Alberta Map
CES Central East Side Map
DT Downtown Map
NE North East/Mississippi Map
NW North West/Nob Hill Map
SE South East Map
OT Old Town Map
P Pearl Map
LC Lloyd Center-ish Map
W Waterfront Map

X Not plotted on PDX Maps

6 Page Number in bold
(alphabetical within category)

Scanning these lists for ideas on where to go to Happy Hour will help you plan your next outing. Sorry – you'll have to get used to referencing the **index in the back for alphabetical listings.**

American

American/NW

- DT **36** 50 Plates
- NE **37** Belly
- SE **38** Belly Timber
- NW **39** Carlyle
- W **40** Chart House
- OT **41** Davis Street
- CES **42** Farm Café
- NE **43** Lincoln
- NW **44** Lucy's Table
- NW **45** Meriwether's
- DT **46** Mez
- DT **47** Mother's
- P **48** Park Kitchen
- NE **49** Soluna
- LC **50** Tabla

Retro/Old School

- DT **51** Daily Grill
- LC **52** Doug Fir
- DT **53** Driftwood Room
- SE **54** Gold Dust
- AL **55** Radio Room
- DT **56** The Original

Seafood

- DT **57** Dan & Louis'
- W **58** Newport Bay
- LC,W **59** Newport Seafood

Southern

- AL **60** Bernie's
- NE **61** Miss Delta
- NW **62** Pope House
- DT **63** Red Star
- LC **64** Tapalaya
- AL **65** Tin Shed

Steak Houses

- DT **66** El Gaucho
- DT **67** Kincaid's
- DT **68** Morton's
- DT **69** Ringside
- X **70** Ringside Glendover
- DT **71** Ruth's Chris

Traditional Classics

- DT **72** Benson Hotel
- DT **73** Heathman*
- DT **74** Huber's
- DT **75** Jake's Famous
- DT **76** Jake's Grill
- DT **77** McCormick&Schmick
- DT **78** Portland City Grill
- DT **79** Stanford's
- NW **80** Uptown Billiards
- P **81** Wilf's

Nice & Casual

- AL **82** Branch Whiskey Bar
- DT **82** Bistro 921
- X **82** Delta Café
- NE **83** Echo
- DT **83** Elephant's Deli
- AL **83** Hilt
- DT **84** Kenny & Zuke's
- NW **84** Melt
- X **84** West Café

= All Night Happy Hour

Beervana

Full Reviews

W 86 B.J.'s Brewhouse
P 87 Bridgeport Brewpub
P 88 Deschute's
P 89 Henry's Tavern
X 90 HUB
NW 91 McTarnahan's
DT 92 Rock Bottom

Half-Pints

X 93 Alameda
NE 93 Amnesia
SE 93 Bridgeport Ale
CES 93 Green Dragon
NW 94 Laurelwood
NE 94 Lompocs
NW 95 Lucky Labs
AL 95 Mashtun
X 95 Raccoon Lodge
P 95 Rogue Ales Pub
CES 96 Roots Brewery
X 96 Salmon Creek
DT 96 Tugboat Brewing
NE 96 Widmer Brewing

Nice Taps

DT 97 Bailey's Taproom
X 97 Belmont Station
X 97 Concordia
X 97 Dublin
NE 97 Hop & Vine
X 97 Horsebrass Pub
CES 97 Produce Row
NE 97 Prost
NE 97 Saraveza

98-100 McMenamins
(They're everywhere!)

"Beer is the reason I get out of bed every afternoon."
—Anonymous

Cocktails & Wine

Wine Country is so close!

Get out and enjoy it! It's beautiful, relaxing, and fun – plus, the wine is delicious. Don't know where to go? Don't worry – The Oregon Wine Country Guidebook makes exploring easy! Photos, maps, fast-find info.

www.winecountryguidebook.com

OREGON
Wine Country
GUIDEBOOK
FREE coupons
Wine MAPS
200+ listings
Cindy Anderson

Contemporary & Eclectic

★Check our **website** when you're headed out for Happy Hour:

- **Top Ten Lists**
- **Ideas & Changes**
- **Maps**
- **Coupons**

* = *All Night Happy Hour*

WWW.HAPPYHOURGUIDEBOOK.COM

International

11

Sports/Water

One of my *very favorite* waterside places to have a drink is **Channel's Edge**, up north in the Bridgeton neighborhood overlooking Hayden Island. Sadly, they don't have a Happy Hour, but they have wine, beer grub, and coffee. Also in the nautical vein, but land-locked, is the **Muddy Rudder**. Check *everything* out on Yelp!

yelp* www.yelp.com

Quick Shots

Casual Quick Shots

Dive Bars

Cheers!

'Burbs

Only the best of the best – Look for the stars!
Take a road trip and you just may find these
places aren't as far away as you might think.
Go on a weekend and go shopping, hit a farmer's
market or take in a movie. Free parking!

'Hoods

- ● Gold dots mark restaurant location

- ★ Places with Weekday Happy Hours going until **7:00pm** are marked with a black star

- ● White dots have limited HH info in this book

Alberta

NORTH
1 MILE

ALBERTA STREET

Lolo's
Bella
Branch
Bernie's

Soi Cowboy

Siam Society

Thai Noon

28th
27th
26th
25th

Alleyway Café

Zaytoon

24th
23rd

Ciao Vito

Mashtun

22nd
21st
20th

Hilt

19th

Zilla Sake

18th
17th
16th
15th

Tin Shed

14th
13th

Radio Room

12th

Alberta Street Public House

11th
10th

16

Central East Side

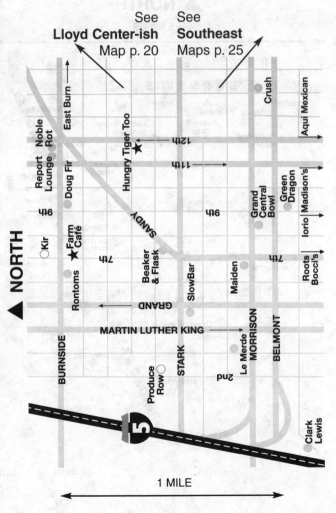

See **Lloyd Center-ish** Map p. 20

See **Southeast** Maps p. 25

East Burn

See **Lloyd Center-ish**

Crush

Aqui Mexican

Noble Rot

Report Lounge

Doug Fir

Hungry Tiger Too

12th

11th

Grand Central Bowl

Green Dragon

9th

9th

Iorio

Madison's

Kir

Farm Café

SANDY

7th

Beaker & Flask

SlowBar

Maiden

7th

Roots

Bocci's

Rontoms

GRAND

▲ NORTH

MARTIN LUTHER KING

BURNSIDE

STARK

Le Merde

MORRISON

BELMONT

Produce Row

2nd

Clark Lewis

5

1 MILE

Downtown (West)

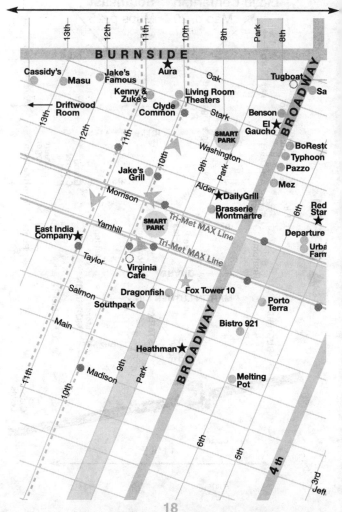

Downtown (East)

▲ NORTH

.25 MILES

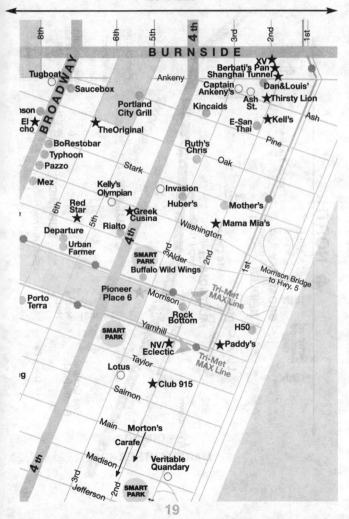

BURNSIDE

8th 6th 5th **4th** 3rd 2nd 1st

BROADWAY

Tugboat

Saucebox

Ankeny

XV

Berbati's Pan
Shanghai Tunnel

Dan&Louis'

Captain
Ankeny's

Ash
St.

Thirsty Lion

nson

El
cho

Portland
City Grill

Kincaids

Kell's

Ash

TheOriginal

E-San
Thai

BoRestobar

Pine

Typhoon

Ruth's
Chris

Pazzo

Stark

Oak

Mez

Kelly's
Olympian

Invasion

6th

Red
Star

5th

Huber's

Mother's

Greek
Cusina

Rialto

Washington

Mama Mia's

Departure

4th

Urban
Farmer

3rd

Alder

2nd

1st

Morrison Bridge
to Hwy. 5

SMART
PARK

Buffalo Wild Wings

Porto
Terra

Pioneer
Place 6

Morrison

Tri-Met
MAX Line

Rock
Bottom

SMART
PARK

Yamhill

H50

NV/
Eclectic

Paddy's

Taylor

Tri-Met
MAX Line

Lotus

Club 915

Salmon

4th

Main

Morton's

3rd

Carafe

Madison

Veritable
Quandary

Jefferson

2nd

SMART
PARK

g

19

Lloyd Center-ish

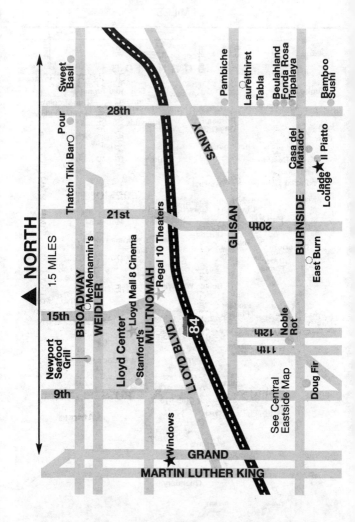

▲ **NORTH**

1.5 MILES

Florida Room

KILLINGSWORTH

Hop & Vine   Chapel Pub   Yakuza

VANCOUVER · WILLIAMS · MARTIN LUTHER KING

INTERSTATE

ALBERTA

5

Trebol

SKIDMORE

Prost!
Casa Naranja
Alibi ★   Equinox
Moloko ★
Lupa   ★ Crow Bar   ★ Lincoln
Mississippi   Miss Delta   ChaChaCha
Station   Lompoc   ★ Anju
Amnesia   5Q   ★ Belly
Por Que No

MISSISSIPPI

FREMONT

County Cork
Perry's, Shaken
Soluna, Alameda

★ Liberty Glass

GREELEY

Alu

Secret
Society

405

Widmer   **RUSSELL**

White   ★ 820   ★★
Eagle   /Mint   Afrique

★ Gotham   Echo
Tavern

NW/Nob Hill
21st/23rd

▲ NORTH
.6 MILES

30

Vaughn

← Meriwether's

Patanegra

Thurman

○ McMenamin's Tavern

Carlyle

New Old Lompoc

Raleigh
Lucky Lab
Quimby

Mayura   Casa del Matador

23rd   22nd   21st   20th   Pettygrove   17th   16th   15th

Overton

Northrup

Café   Marshall
Reese   405   LOVEJOY

Laurelwood   Kearney
NW ★
Santa Fe   Serrato   Café Nell
    Mingo   Johnson
Jo-Bar   21stAve.   Melt
    Voicebox   Lucy's Table   Irving
    Gypsy ○   Cinema 21
23 Hoyt ★ ○ Ram's Head   Muu-Muu's   Hoyt
    North45   V&P Pope House ★   Sweet Basil

GLISAN
Bartini ○ Blue Moon   Mission ★
    Flanders
M Bar ○   Basta's
Cha
EVERETT

Limo   Davis
Uptown Elephant's
Sal's ★ Deli   Matador Couch
    Ringside   BURNSIDE
    Agency

405

Old Town
a.k.a. Happy Hour Heaven 'til 7:00!

▲ **NORTH**
.25 MILES

▲ NORTH

BURNSIDE

BROADWAY

1st
2nd
3rd
4th
5th
6th
7th
8th
Park

Everett
Davis
Couch
Ankeny
Ash

SMALL PARK

McFadden's
Hobo's
Pala
Ping
Crown Room
East
Davis St. Tavern
Gilt Club
Park Kitchen
Chez Joly
Tugboat

Berbati's Pan
XV
Shanghai Tunnel
Dan&Louis'
Thirsty Lion
Captain Ankeny's
Ash St.
Kell's
Kincaids
E-San Thai
Saucebox
Portland City Grill
The Original
Benson
El Gaucho

Pearl District

▲ NORTH

.5 MILES

Metrovino

Marshall

Bridgeport

Seres ★

LOVEJOY

On Deck

Fenouil

Kearney

14th

Johnson

13th

12th

11th

10th

9th

Bay 13

Irving

Paragon ○

Fratelli/
BarDué

Low
Brow ○

Hoyt

★ Holden's
Touché

Oba! ●

★ Camellia's

GLISAN

Andina

Silk ★

Rogue
Brewery ○

Vino
Paradiso ○

Flanders

★ Isabel

50 Plates ●

Bluehour ●

Teardrop
Lounge ★

Life of Riley

★

EVERETT

○ Jinx
○ Vault

★ Jimmy
Mak's

Davis

Deschutes

★ SushiLand

PFChang's

★ Blitz

Couch

Ten01

★ Candy

Henry's ●

BURNSIDE

24

Southeast

Please note: Maps and streets do not align.

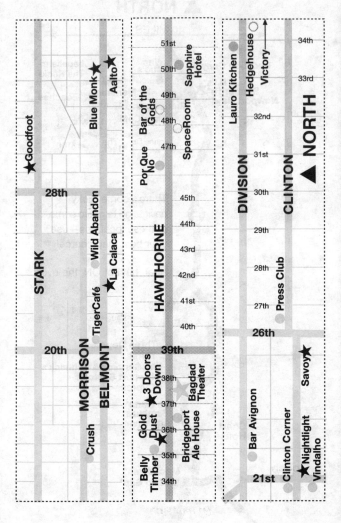

★ Goodfoot

★ Blue Monk

★ Aalto

28th

STARK

Wild Abandon

La Calaca

TigerCafé

MORRISON

BELMONT

20th

Crush

51st

Sapphire Hotel

50th

Bar of the Gods

49th

48th

SpaceRoom

47th

Por Que No

45th

44th

HAWTHORNE

43rd

42nd

41st

40th

39th

★ 3 Doors Down

38th

Bagdad Theater

37th

Bridgeport Ale House

36th

Belly Timber

Gold Dust ★

35th

34th

Lauro Kitchen

Hedgehouse ○

Victory →

34th

33rd

32nd

NORTH

DIVISION

31st

CLINTON

30th

▲ NORTH

29th

28th

Press Club

27th

26th

Savoy ★

Bar Avignon

Clinton Corner

★ Nightlight

Vindalho

21st

25

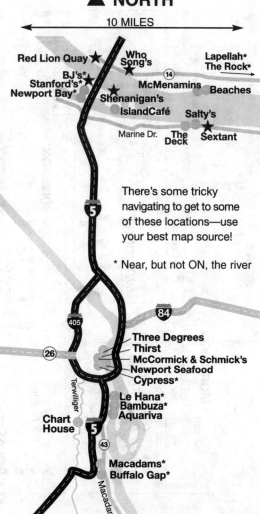

Beervana

(Near Downtown)

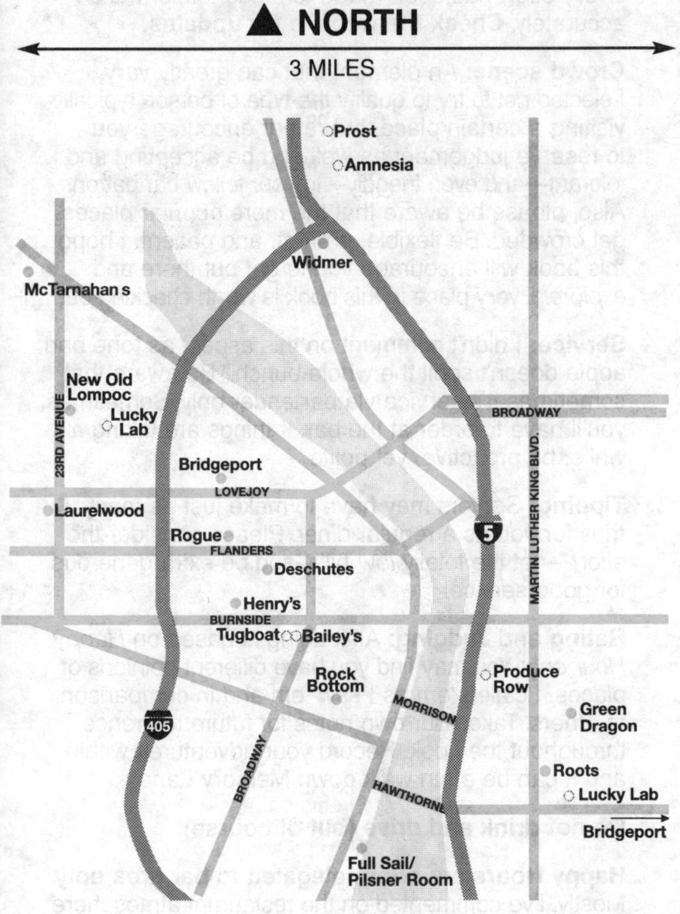

▲ **NORTH**

◄─────── 3 MILES ───────►

Prost

Amnesia

Widmer

McTarnahan's

New Old Lompoc

Lucky Lab

BROADWAY

Bridgeport

LOVEJOY

23RD AVENUE

Laurelwood

Rogue

FLANDERS

MARTIN LUTHER KING BLVD.

5

Deschutes

Henry's

BURNSIDE

Tugboat ∞ Bailey's

Rock Bottom

Produce Row

MORRISON

Green Dragon

405

Roots

Lucky Lab

BROADWAY

HAWTHORNE

Bridgeport

Full Sail/ Pilsner Room

Notes and Disclaimers

Accuracy of information: Things change! Graciously accept this fluidity and adjust your attitude accordingly. As of this writing, the information herein is current. Every effort has been made to present information accurately. **Check the website for updates.**

Crowd scene: An element that can greatly vary. I elected not to try to qualify the type of person typically visiting a certain place, but rather encourage you to reserve judgement as well and be accepting and tolerant—and even friendly—to your fellow bar patrons. Also, please be aware that the more popular places get crowded. Be flexible, prompt, and patient. I hope this book will encourage you to get out there and *explore!* Every place in this book is worth checking out.

Service: I didn't comment on this aspect as "one bad apple doesn't spoil the whole bunch." Be aware that sometimes it's service via bartender only. Sometimes, you'll have to order at the bar. If things are taking a while, be proactive, yet polite.

Tipping: Servers may have to make just as many trips for you as a regular diner. Please consider the effort—not the totally *low* bill—and be extra-generous for good service!

Rating and Judging: All judging is based on *Happy Hour only*. You may find you have different opinions of places. I called 'em as I saw 'em and in comparison to others. Take your own notes for future reference throughout the book. Record your adventures within and it can be a fun walk down Memory Lane!

Do not drink and drive (but of course).

Happy Hours are often relegated to bar area only. Mostly, I've commented on the restaurant atmosphere overall, including outdoor seating (which may not always be available to the Happy Hour crowd). Ask before you are seated to confirm available service.

Reviews

About Food Ratings

It's a formula of taste + variety vs. discounts:

1 = Limited food alternatives
A place could have sub-par food, but more than likely a 1 rating means a limited menu, small portions, or a meager price break during Happy Hour compared to other times of the day.

2 = Pretty decent deals and/or selections
Places rated with a 2 offer basic good food at lower Happy Hour prices. Most places will fall into this category. Some high-end restaurants end up with only 2's as well, due to the higher expense for what you get.

3 = Exceptionally delicious and discounted
These restaurants offer numerous menu items with decent-sized portions, have at least one healthier alternative, their food is exceptionally tasty or unique, *and* is noticeably discounted.

About Drinks

Size *does* matter in pours of shots and glasses, but quality and price matter too:

0 = **No drink discount**
Sadly, not every bar/restaurant offers drink discounts at Happy Hour (which technically goes against the definition of the term); however, they make us quite happy with their food. And hey, if you don't want to drink, it makes no difference.

1 = **Limited drink selection and/or discount**
Only one point for bars offering a small discount or limited drink choices.

2 = **Pretty decent deals and/or selections**
For basic, somewhat limited, drink specials.

3 = **Extra-cheap drinks and/or several alternatives**
A 3 is for bars offering an extra-big discount, unique options and/or have good specials on beer, wine, wells *and* cocktails.

About Atmosphere

Different places appeal to different people for different reasons. I look for signs of good restaurant design and my judgments are based on perceived aesthetic quality.

1 = Very basic/nothing special
Not much attention given to decorating or creating a unique atmosphere. Borderline dive bar.

2 = Casual style
A nice place, but design concept not taken very far.

3 = Upscale, unusual decor or nice view
Reflects a creative effort that enhances the customer's experience.

Overall, I didn't address how crowded bars are. Some of the best places were quite empty, which is unbelievable to me. Try new spots— you can enjoy a nice restaurant meal for a fraction of dinner prices. People of Portland: *Get out there and enjoy!*

Other Information

BIG number
indicates
overall
rating/
score

7

TOP TEN FAVORITE!

Indicates my personal "Top Ten"
favorites (hard to do and by no
means all)! I favor visual stunners.

Food Deals	2
Drink Specials +	2
Atmosphere +	2
	———
=	7?

Magic Point!

A note about the "Magic Point" system:

The Magic Point is an arbitrary point that I
sometimes threw into the final score to account
for the synergistic effect of the whole being
greater than the sum of its parts. I chose to use
only *whole numbers* when rating each category
of food, drink, or atmosphere, and since I didn't
use half-points, sometimes the tallied score just
didn't quite do the bar justice. Plus I wanted
some places to get perfect 10's.

Gold Star:
Indicates overall rating
of a perfect **10**

Silver Star:
Indicates overall rating
of a near-perfect **9**
(note that not all "9's"
quite merit a silver star)

A small, solid gold star indicates places
that would be perfect except they don't
offer any drink specials.

★ Small black star indicates extended hours.
All night Sundays of particular note!

✛ Sometimes I just have to say "WOW!"
It's kinda like an "A+."

American Style

American/NW
Old-School/Retro
Steaks
Seafood
Southern Style
Traditional Classics

Restaurants in this section will cover a wide variety of places serving mainly American food. Full page reviews include many of the area's best restaurants. The shorter reviews highlight some of the more casual places, or those without much of a discount at Happy Hour. Of course, you'll find some interesting international influences along the way – after all, we're living in a melting pot!

50 Plates

9

●●●●●●●●●●●●●●●●●●●●●●●●●●

Pearl Map
333 NW 13th
(503) 228-5050
www.50plates.com

Happy Hours
3:00–6:00pm Daily; Sun-Thurs 9:00pm-close
10:00pm-close Fri-Sat

Food Deals 3
$2.50–$5.00
Rotating samplings of the 50 states with smaller,
discounted portions of their regular appetizers:
five kinds of sammies, several salads, fries,
clams, shrimp or mussels. Free tasters too.

Drink Specials 2
$5.00 red or white wine
$5.00 wide selection of cocktails

Atmosphere 3
Contemporary spin on diner-style chic; simple,
square and stark with neutrals; formica cocktail
tables, dark woods and creamy tiled bar. Long
open kitchen and fun outdoor patio tables.

Date visited: _____

Went with: _____

Notes: _____

_____

_____

My rating: _____

Belly

North/NE Map
3500 NE MLK Blvd
(503) 249-9763
www.bellyrestaurant.com

Happy Hours
5:00–7:00pm Tues–Sat
★ Happy Hour food prices at the bar top all times!

Food Deals 3
$3.00–$6.00
Comfort food done right: wood-fired pizza, fries,
house-ground burger, salad, soup, pork belly
sandwich, grilled meatballs, hush puppies.

Drink Specials 3
$3.00 NW microbrews; $5.00 house wines
$5.00 barmaster's concoction of the day

Atmosphere 3
Comfortable and friendly, fresh and new with
a big, open room and open kitchen; kind of an
"urban rustic" charm with touches of down-home
farm life on the fancy side.

Date visited: _____

Went with: _____

Notes: _____

_____

_____

My rating: _____

Belly Timber

• • • • • • • • • • • • • • • •

Southeast Map
3257 SE Hawthorne
(503) 235-3277
www.bellytimberrestaurant.com

Happy Hours
5:00pm–6:30pm Tues–Sun

Food Deals 3
$2.00–$6.00; $20.00 3-course prixe fixe menu.
Changing seasonal menu with themes like
"Whole Hog" and an array of pork specialties.
Go hog wild with fancy, foodie prixe fixe menu!

Drink Specials 3
$3.00 microbrews; $4.00 red or white wine
$5.00 cocktails (like a Mary Pickford, daiquiri,
or a Lime Rickey)

Atmosphere 3+
An absolutely gorgeous and giant Victorian
home on Hawthorne houses this incredibly
charming, warm, and inviting restaurant. LOVE!

Date visited: ....
Went with: ....
Notes: ....
....
....

My rating: ....

Carlyle

NW/Nob Hill Map
1632 NW Thurman
(503) 595-1782
www.carlylerestaurant.com

Happy Hours
4:00-6:30pm Mon–Fri

Food Deals 2
$1.00–$13.00 ($3.00 off regular menu prices).
High-end restaurant and high-quality food, but
on the pricey side: oysters on the half-shell, ribs,
soup, carpaccio, tempura squash, burgers.

Drink Specials 2
$3.00 drafts; $4.00 wine

Atmosphere 3
Sleek and neat with a gorgeous cherry wood bar;
chic, city-style simplicity with some old-school
retro mixed in; high girdered black ceiling and
huge windows. Very nice.

Date visited: _____

Went with: _____

Notes: _____

_____

_____

My rating: _____

Chart House

●●●●●●●●●●●●●●●●●●●

Warterfront Map (Near OHSU)
5700 SW Terwilliger Blvd
(503) 246-6963
www.chart-house.com

Happy Hours
4:00–7:00pm Mon-Fri

Food Deals 3
$3.00–$5.00
Three options at $3.00, $4.00 or $5.00 each:
bruschetta, artichoke hearts, firecracker shrimp,
ahi tuna, prime rib sliders, fish tacos and oysters.

Drink Specials 3
$4.00 selection of red or white wines, draft beer
or wells; $5.00 cocktails; $6.00 martinis

Atmosphere 3
Wow! Definitely one of the best views in the city,
especially on a clear day when you can see Mt.
Hood *and* Mt. Adams through the floor-to-ceiling,
wall-to-wall windows. Happy Hour is downstairs in
the lounge. Fireplace for winter. Free valet parking.

Date visited: ⟋⟍⟋⟍⟋⟍⟋⟍⟋⟍⟋⟍⟋⟍⟋⟍⟋⟍⟋⟍

Went with: ⟋⟍⟋⟍⟋⟍⟋⟍⟋⟍⟋⟍⟋⟍⟋⟍⟋⟍⟋⟍

Notes: ⟋⟍⟋⟍⟋⟍⟋⟍⟋⟍⟋⟍⟋⟍⟋⟍⟋⟍⟋⟍⟋⟍⟋⟍

⟋⟍⟋⟍⟋⟍⟋⟍⟋⟍⟋⟍⟋⟍⟋⟍⟋⟍⟋⟍⟋⟍⟋⟍⟋⟍⟋⟍

⟋⟍⟋⟍⟋⟍⟋⟍⟋⟍⟋⟍⟋⟍⟋⟍⟋⟍⟋⟍⟋⟍⟋⟍⟋⟍⟋⟍

My rating: ⟋⟍⟋⟍⟋⟍⟋⟍

Davis Street Tavern

9

Old Town Map
500 NW Davis Street
(503) 505-5050
www.davisstreettavern.com

Happy Hours
4:00–6:30pm Mon–Sat

Food Deals 3
$3.00–$6.00
Stepped-up, big bar menu includes oysters and mussels, burgers and brats, fish tacos, salads, mac & cheese, seared albacore, BBQ sandwich.

Drink Specials 2
$4.00 beer; $5.00–$6.00 wines

Atmosphere 3
Full of light and Old Town warehouse character, this warm and classy tavern makes for a most perfect spot to congregate and satiate. Brick walls, soaring wood-beamed ceilings, wooden z-shaped bar and giant medieval chandeliers.

Date visited: _____

Went with: _____

Notes: _____

_____

_____

My rating: _____

The Farm Café

Central East Side Map
10 SE 7th Ave
(503) 736-3276
www.thefarmcafe.com

Happy Hours
5:00–6:30pm Mon–Fri

Food Deals 3
$2.00–$4.00
Short but sweet menu – fresh goodies change
often and with the seasons: hummus plate, wings,
mountain-o-fries, crostini, salads, soup.

Drink Specials 2
$1.00 off draft beer; $4.00 red and white wines

Atmosphere 3+
High-level cuteness alert! Located in a renovated,
old Victorian home dripping with charm. Romantic
and intimate with several meandering, cozy dining
rooms. Big seasonal patio and back bar.

Date visited: _____

Went with: _____

Notes: _____

_____

_____

My rating: _____

Lincoln

● ●

NE Map
3808 N Williams, #127
(503) 288-6200
www.lincolnpdx.com

Happy Hours
5:30–7:00pm Tues–Fri

Food Deals 3
$2.00–$6.00
Americana home cooking with NW culinary bent
and seasonal, funky-fresh menu: crispy fritters,
patty melt, fresh greens, flatbread, baked eggs.

Drink Specials 3
$3.00 microbrews; $4.00 house wines
$5.00 wells; $6.00 specialty cocktail

Atmosphere 3
Located in the northside's HUB building, a strip
of chic, renovated loft-style warehouse spaces.
Interior is on the more basic side of industrial
chic, but warmth is added via dark-red walls,
natural woods, friendly staff and votive candles.

Date visited: ....

Went with: ....

Notes: ....

....

....

My rating: ....

Lucy's Table

704 NW 21st Ave.
(503) 226-6126
www.lucystable.com

Happy Hours
5:00–6:30pm Mon–Fri

Food Deals 3
$3.00–$4.00
Half-off delicious bar menu that changes somewhat seasonally: Goat cheese ravioli, ribs, mixed
greens or beet salad, oysters, Lucy's corndogs.

Drink Specials 3
$3.00 draft beer; $4.00 well drinks
$4.00 select red and white wine; $4.00 cocktails

Atmosphere 3
Small bar area with a Pottery Barn-ish simplicity.
Very nice and appealing space where you'll be
focusing on the great food more than anything!
Gets crowded, so go early.

Date visited: _____

Went with: _____

Notes: _____

_____

_____

My rating: _____

Meriwether's

NW/Nob Hill Map
2601 NW Vaughn
(503) 228-1250
www.meriwethersnw.com

Happy Hours
3:00-6:00pm Daily

Food Deals 3
$2.00–$10.00
Pretty much half-off their extensive bar menu:
current offerings include chickpea fritters, warm
olives, spicy almonds, soup, salads, cauliflower
gratin, flatbread, fries, cheddar burger, pulled
pork sandwich, pizza.

Drink Specials 2
$3.00 draft beer; $5.00 select wine

Atmosphere 3+
Built on the site of the 1905 World's Fair. Their
historic and stately interior exudes a warm and
hospitable countryside inn quality. Impressive!

Date visited: _____

Went with: _____

Notes: _____

_____

_____

My rating: _____

Mez on Broadway

• •

Downtown (East) Map
520 SW Broadway
(503) 552-2220
www.marriottportland.com/dining

Happy Hours
4:00–6:00pm Daily

Food Deals 3
$2.50–$4.50
Half-off high-quality bar menu: pear salad, pizza,
turkey melt, pork sliders, calamari, fries, quesadilla,
Caesar salad, tempura asparagus.

Drink Specials 0
Sadly, no drink specials

Atmosphere 3
Climb up the grand, circular staircase up to the
gallery-like mezzanine level of the Marriott. Rich
dark woods, decorative moldings, and a rotating
artist showcase set the stage for elegance, but
the bar isn't *that* fancy.

Date visited: ....

Went with: ....

Notes: ....

....

....

My rating: ....

Mother's

● ●

212 SW Stark
(503) 464-1122
www.mothersbistro.com

Happy Hours
3:00–6:00pm Tues–Fri

Food Deals 2
$3.00
Fried ravioli, chicken quesadilla, mini-burgers,
deviled eggs, hummus plate, chopped liver,
and little teenie weenies.

Drink Specials 3
$3.00 microbrew pints; $3.00 wells
$5.00 array of infused cocktails

Atmosphere 2
Their "Velvet Lounge" bar area steps back in
time and looks much like a wealthy, Southern
grandmother's home. Ornate gilded mirrors,
chandeliers, and flocked wallpaper everywhere.

Date visited: _____

Went with: _____

Notes: _____

_____

_____

My rating: _____

Park Kitchen

• •

Old Town Map
422 NW 8th Ave
(503) 223-7275
www.parkkitchen.com

Happy Hours
5:00–7:00pm Mon–Sat

Food Deals 2
$8.00
Seasonal changes with Americana-nouveau small plates like fried green beans with bacon and tarragon, smoked cod with pickled elderberries or shaved apple, manchego & hazelnuts.

Drink Specials 2
$5.00 wines; $5.00 cocktails (retro selections)

Atmosphere 3
Cute and cozy bistro across from the park with café tables outside, but sadly, Happy Hour go-ers are relegated to the bar. Don't worry – you'll still experience the sweet, subdued, almost-country respite inside.

Date visited: ....

Went with: ....

Notes: ....

....

....

My rating: ....

Soluna Grill

••••••••••••••••••••••••••

NE Map
4440 NE Fremont
(971) 222-3433
www.solunagrill.com

Happy Hours
3:00–6:00 Mon–Sat

Food Deals 3
$3.00–$6.00
Well-studied food mix that changes somewhat
seasonally: goat cheese stuffed artichoke hearts,
mushroom and cream cheese potstickers, chips,
spiced green beans, 1/2 lb. burger, gnocchi.

Drink Specials 1
$1.00 off beer, wine and wells

Atmosphere 3
A lunar-scene painting with warm, sunny tones
anchors the dining room which is bathed in light
from streetside windows. Nighttime brings out
the cool-but-subtle light fixtures and candles.

Date visited: _____

Went with: _____

Notes: _____

....

_____

My rating: _____

Tabla

● ●

Lloyd Center-ish Map
200 NE 28th Ave
(503) 238-3777
www.tabla-restaurant.com

Happy Hours
5:00–6:30pm Daily

Food Deals 3
$6.00–$7.00
One of the Northwest's best offers Happy Hour at the bar with a fresh, seasonal menu which changes weekly. Always high-quality with items like the Tabla ravioli, salads or a cheese plate.

Drink Specials 2
$3.50 drafts; $5.00–$6.50 red or white house wine
$5.00 special cocktail

Atmosphere 3
Simple, home-style decor with banquette seating, flowers on tables and at windows, plus original art. Not suitable for groups as Happy Hour is at bar only (plus seasonal sidewalk seating).

Date visited: _____

Went with: _____

Notes: _____

_____

_____

My rating: _____

Daily Grill

● ●

Downtown (West) Map
750 SW Alder
(503) 294-7001
www.westinportland.com/dailygrill

Happy Hours
4:00–7:00pm Mon–Fri

Food Deals 3
$2.95–$3.95
Kobe beef "sidekick" sliders, seared ahi, hummus,
mac & cheese, mini pot-pies, spinach-artichoke
dip, calamari, quesadilla.

Drink Specials 2
$1.00 off beer; $2.00 off all wine
$5.50 wells; $6.00 premium martini

Atmosphere 3
Bogart-y '40s-style upscale hotel bar; deep, warm
cranberry walls, dark woods and thick moldings;
leather booths with cocktail tables.

Date visited: ....
Went with: ....
Notes: ....
....
....

My rating: ....

Doug Fir

Lloyd Center-ish Map
830 E Burnside
(503) 231-9663
www.dougfirlounge.com

Happy Hours
3:00–6:00pm Daily

Food Deals 2
$3.00
Plentiful portions of comfort food: cheeseburger, mashers and gravy, croque monsieur, tomato soup, salads, bread pudding, cheese fries, artichoke & spinach dip, chicken strips.

Drink Specials 3
$3.00 drafts, house wine and wells

Atmosphere 3
Twin Peaks meets the Sinatra 50's in classy-kitsch Northwest lodge theme; couch pits for groups; outdoor patio seating. Order at the bar. Great place to see bands downstairs! Also fun to stay at neighboring Jupiter Hotel.

Date visited: _____

Went with: _____

Notes: _____

_____

_____

My rating: _____

Driftwood Room

● ●

Downtown (West) Map
729 SW 15th Ave.
(503) 223-6311
www.hoteldeluxeportland.com

Happy Hours
3:00–6:00pm and 9:00pm–close Daily

Food Deals 3
$2.50–$5.00
Big and outstanding menu: pork loin sandwich,
sizzling forest mushrooms, fried oysters, crab
cakes, mac & cheese, portobello burger, fries.

Drink Specials 1
$5.00 house wine, $5.00 champagne cocktail

Atmosphere 3
Off the *very* impressive grand lobby of the Hotel
deLuxe, the Driftwood has a dark, discreet, and
fancy ratpack appeal in a kidney-shaped, dimly-
lit, wooden room with NW touches. Very unique
and upscale-retro-cool ambiance.

Date visited: _____

Went with: _____

Notes: _____

_____

_____

My rating: _____

Gold Dust Meridian

8

3267 SE Hawthorne Blvd
(503) 239-1143
www.golddustmeridian.com

Happy Hours
★2:00–8:00pm Daily

Food Deals 3
$3.00–$6.00
Menu follows period style and includes bar olives, deviled eggs, grilled cheese trio (served with soup and salad), fritters, salami plate, mac & cheese, shrimp brochette, mussels & clams.

Drink Specials 1
50 cents off pints or wells; $1.00 off wine

Atmosphere 3
Marathon Happy Hour joint with a dark interior that is steeped deep in authentic retro charm and is at once swanky, chill, and ultra-cool.

Date visited: ....

Went with: ....

Notes: ....

....

....

My rating: ....

Radio Room

• •

Alberta Map
1101 NE Alberta St
(503) 287-2346

Happy Hours
3:00–6:00pm and 11:00pm–close (food) Daily

Food Deals 2
$3.00–$5.50
Sticks with their somewhat 50s-American theme with food that sticks to the ribs: burgers, fries, mac & cheese, onion rings, croque monsieur or fried egg & bacon sandwiches, salads and soups.

Drink Specials 2
$2.75 microbrews; $6.00 wine of the week
$2.75 wells; $7.00 cocktail

Atmosphere 3
All-out sleek and mod interior fitting of big-city style standards; both upper *and* lower outdoor decks with bright blue umbrellas and big stone firepit; huge bar with open garage doors; cool movie posters; radio room rumored in rear.

Date visited: _____

Went with: _____

Notes: _____

_____

_____

My rating: _____

The Original

Downtown Map
300 SW 6th Ave.
(503) 546.2666
www.originaldinerant.com

Happy Hours
3:00–6:00pm ('til 8:00pm at the bar) Daily

Food Deals 3
$1.00–$5.00
American diner food with some Happy Hour
oddities: voodoo donut burger, fried bologna,
pigs in a blanket, fritters, donuts, poptarts.

Drink Specials 2
$1.00 PBR; $3.00 wines; $4.00 Rose's daily punch

Atmosphere 3
Very mod, retro *and* contemporary restaurant/
diner (aka "dinerant"). Amazingly giant, floor-to-
ceiling, wall-to-wall windows that are two stories
high, and run the length of the building. Sleek
interior blends downtown, city-cool with the
charm of 1950s greasy spoon lunch counters.

Date visited:

Went with:

Notes:

My rating:

SEAFOOD
Dan & Louis' Oyster Bar

Old Town Map
208 SW Ankeny
(503) 227-5906
www.danandlouis.com

Happy Hours
4:00–6:00pm Mon–Fri

Food Deals 2
$1.95–$4.95
Cajun pan-fried oysters, oyster sliders, half-pound cheeseburger, fish tacos, fries, oysters on the half-shell $15.95/dozen.

Drink Specials 0
Sadly, no drink specials

Atmosphere 3
Totally different with small-town, East-Coast, casual crabbing charm. Worth ducking in from the alley to this cozy, candlelit, ship-like hideaway. Loaded with portside personality.

Date visited: _____

Went with: _____

Notes: _____

_____

_____

My rating: _____

Newport Bay

9

Portland/Jantzen Beach
11950 N Center Ave.; (503) 283-3474
Beaverton
2865 NW Town Center Loop; (503) 645-2526
Gresham
2757 SE Burnside; (503) 661-2722
Tigard
9699 SW Washington Sq. Rd.; (503) 620-3474
Vancouver
7717 NE Vancouver Plaza Dr.; (360) 896-9795
www.newportbay.com

Happy Hours
3:00–7:00pm and 9:00pm to close Daily

Food Deals 3
$1.99–$3.99
A very similar line-up as Newport Seafood Grill.

Drink Specials 2 Drink specials added!
Usually $3.50 microbrews, wine and wells

Atmosphere 3
Cape Cod boater-casual with upscale style.

Date visited: _____

Went with: _____

Notes: _____

_____

_____

My rating: _____

Newport Seafood Grill

• •

9

1200 NE Broadway
(503) 493-0100
Portland Waterfront (see page 236)
Tigard
10935 SW 68th Parkway; (503) 245-3474
www.newportseafoodgrill.com

Happy Hours
3:00–6:00pm Daily

Food Deals 3
$1.95–$3.95
15 varied menu items including clam chowder,
fish & chips, salads, sushi rolls, crab cakes, fish
tacos, sliders, crab cakes, seafood gumbo.

Drink Specials 2
Most have drink specials now!
Usually $3.50 microbrews, wine and wells

Atmosphere 3
Popular, big, and bustling bar area. Upscale
restaurant conveniently located near Lloyd
Center Mall and the movie theaters.

Date visited: _____

Went with: _____

Notes: _____

_____

_____

My rating: _____

Bernie's Southern Bistro

9

• •

Alberta Map
2904 NE Alberta
(503) 282-9864
www.berniesbistro.com

Happy Hours
4:00–6:00pm Tues–Sat

Food Deals 3
$3.00
Gourmet southern samplers including Po' Boys,
fried green tomatoes, red beans & rice, veggie
salad, sweet potato fries, mac & cheese, fried
pickles, meatloaf sandwich, hush puppies.

Drink Specials 2
$4.00 house wines; $5.00 cocktail specials

Atmosphere 3
Serene outdoor garden patio, and they even let
you sit outside for Happy Hour. Quite lovely!
Simple, fine-dining, romantic interior. Casual bar.

Date visited: _____

Went with: _____

Notes: _____

_____

_____

My rating: _____

Miss Delta

●●●●●●●●●●●●●●●●●●●●●

3950 N Mississippi Ave.
(503) 287-7629
www.missdeltapdx.net

Happy Hours
5:00–6:00pm and 10:00pm–close Daily

Food Deals 2
$2.00–$5.00
Take a side: collard greens, red beans & rice,
mashed potatoes, mac & cheese, or black-eyed
peas. Or try sweet potato fries, hush puppies,
corn bread muffin, fritters or salad. $6 for a mix!

Drink Specials 2
$3.00 pints; $3.50 wells; $1.00 off cocktails

Atmosphere 2
Quaint, old-time N'awlins saloon style. Small
room with long bar with brick walls, rustic wood
floors, antique hanging lamps and for added
effect, mason jar candles.

Date visited: _____

Went with: _____

Notes: _____

_____

_____

My rating: _____

The Pope House

● ●

NW/Nob Hill Map
2075 NW Glisan
(503) 222-1056
www.popehouselounge.com

Happy Hours
4:00–7:00pm Tues–Sat; 4:00pm–mid Sunday★

Food Deals 3
$4.00–$5.00
Yes! Frito Pie! Plus a delicious array of grilled
tea sandwiches, fritters, pulled pork quesadilla.

Drink Specials 3
$3.00 beer; $4.00 house wines and cocktails

Atmosphere 3
Lots to live up to with taking over the old Brazen
Bean house, but the new owners have done it
right and turned this wonderful Victorian house
into a refined and welcoming southern home.
Several parlor-like dining/drinking rooms, social
central bar, and lots and lots of whiskey to boot!

Date visited: ....

Went with: ....

Notes: ....

....

....

My rating: ....

SOUTHERN
Red Star Tavern

503 SW Alder
(503) 222-0005
www.redstartavern.com

Happy Hours
4:00–8:00pm Daily★

Food Deals 3
$3.00
Bigger than Texas array of bar bites: BBQ wings, hushpuppies; fish, veggie or beef tacos; pork, meatloaf or ham sliders; beef w/ onions & gravy, fries, salads, nachos, oysters, popcorn.

Drink Specials 3
$3.00 beer, wine and wells
$5.00 specialty cocktails

Atmosphere 3
Romantic and upscale with touch of rustic charm; interesting street-scape viewing; big booth options for some serious lounging.
To recap: 3 dollars, 4 hours, 7 days a week!

Date visited: _____

Went with: _____

Notes: _____

_____

_____

My rating: _____

Tapalaya

●●●●●●●●●●●●●●●●●●●●●●

Lloyd Center-ish Map
28 NE 28th Ave
(503) 232-6652
www.tapalaya.com

Happy Hours
4:30–6:00 Daily
All night Wednesdays if you ride your bike there.

Food Deals 2
$2.00–$5.00
Tapas/bites of New Orleans menu just about
perfect for getting one of everything to share,
like fried pickles, sliders, mac & cheese, beignets.

Drink Specials 3+
$3.00 drafts; $4.00 red or white wine
$2.00 martinis and $3.00 hurricanes (YES!)

Atmosphere 3
Laissez les bon temps rouler! Not wild, but fun;
more cozy and cute; neighborhoody and nice.
Live music Thursdays – check calendar.

Date visited: _____

Went with: _____

Notes: _____

_____

_____

My rating: _____

Tin Shed

● ● ● ● ● ● ● ● ● ● ● ● ● ● ● ● ● ● ● ●

Alberta Map
1438 NE Alberta
(503) 288-6966
www.tinshedgardencafe.com

Happy Hours
3:00–6:00pm and 9:00–10:00pm Mon–Sat;
3:00pm–10:00pm Sundays★

Food Deals 3
$2.00–$5.50
Limited, but fresh and oh-so-tasty! Get the
Berry Garcia Quesadilla! There's also a special
mac & cheese of the day, fish tacos, burger,
shed salad, nachos and artichoke dip.

Drink Specials 3
$3.00 microbrews; $3.00 wine
$5.00 specialty drinks

Atmosphere 2
Rustic corrugated tin walls; colorful & bright
elsewhere. Loud interior; big and wonderful
outdoor garden café with fireplace.

Date visited: _____

Went with: _____

Notes: _____

_____

_____

My rating: _____

El Gaucho

319 SW Broadway
(503) 227-8794
www.elgaucho.com

Happy Hours
5:00–7:00pm and 10:00pm–close Mon–Sat

Food Deals 3
$6.00–$14.00
Yay!! A real Happy Hour, albeit a touch on the
spendy side: steak frites, cheddar bacon burger,
beef short ribs, salads, and cheese plates.

Drink Specials 2
$4.00 beer; $5.00 red or white wine
$6.00 cosmos

Atmosphere 3
Notably classy, classic steakhouse. Enjoy a
memorable evening in their dramatic lounge.
See a celebrity or just feel like one yourself.
(Author note: I think they have the best dinner
steak in the city. Worth the occasional splurge!)

Date visited: _____

Went with: _____

Notes: _____

_____

_____

My rating: _____

STEAKHOUSE
Kincaid's

●●●●●●●●●●●●●●●●●

Downtown (East) Map
121 SW 3rd Ave.
(503) 223-6200
www.kincaids.com

Happy Hours
4:00–6:00pm and 9:00pm–close Mon–Sat
★ All day Sunday 11:00am–10:00pm

Food Deals 3
$4.00-$7.00
1/2 off giant list of 18 appetizers: Kobe beef
sliders, crab & artichoke dip, steak bites, fries,
baked brie, calamari, tostada, wings, rings,
crab cakes, prawns, scallops, and oysters.

Drink Specials 3
$4.00 for your choice of any draft beer,
house red or white wine; margaritas or mojitos

Atmosphere 3
Located in Embassy Suites; elegant restaurant
dining on the cheap; rich mahongany wood and
private booth seating; hi-def TVs.

Date visited: ....

Went with: ....

Notes: ....

....

....

My rating: ....

Morton's

●●●●●●●●●●●●●●●●●●●

Downtown Map
213 SW Clay St
(503) 248-2100
www.mortons.com

Happy Hours
5:00–6:30pm and 9:00pm–close Daily

Food Deals 3
$5.00
They've really quite outdone themselves – steak lovers, rejoice! You'll get a platter of four steak sandwiches, three 5" high slider burgers or four salad wedge bites; crab cakes, artichoke dip, fries.

Drink Specials 3
$4.00 drafts; $5.00 red and white wines
$7.00 martinis (on the spendy side, but good!)

Atmosphere 3
I'm so HAPPY Morton's has a new Happy Hour! And oh, what a joyous one it is indeed. Small bar area will fill up fast, so grab a table early. Enjoy the dark, rich ambiance in the bar area of this top-notch, manly-man steakhouse near Keller.

Date visited: _____

Went with: _____

Notes: _____

_____

_____

My rating: _____

STEAKHOUSE
Ringside Downtown

• •

NW/Nob Hill Map
2165 NW Burnside
(503) 223-1513
www.ringsidesteakhouse.com

Happy Hours
9:45pm–close Daily
4:00–6:00 pm Sundays

Food Deals 3+
$2.25 each
Steak bites (YUM!), fish bites, wings, prime rib, ground steak burger, chili poppers, garlic bread, Caesars, fried oysters & shooters.

Drink Specials 0
Sadly, no drink specials

Atmosphere 3
WOW! Now *this* is "old-school!" Fiery, 40's-style, atmospheric, wrap-around patron bar with bartender pit showcasing flaming Spanish coffee-making artistry.

Date visited: _____

Went with: _____

Notes: _____

_____

_____

My rating: _____

STEAKHOUSE

Ringside Glendover

● ●

Glendover (Not on map)
14021 NE Glisan
503-255-0750
www.ringsidesteakhouse.com

Happy Hours
3:00–6:00 pm and 8:30pm–close Daily

Food Deals 3
$2.25-4.95
15 menu items: steak bites (YUM!), calamari,
wings, prime rib dip, crab cake, ground steak
burger, chili poppers, garlic bread, Caesar salad,
oysters on the half shell, steamed clams.

Drink Specials 3
$4.00 microbrew draft beers, red or white wine,
select well drinks, margaritas or Manhattan

Atmosphere 2
Less dramatic, but bigger and more open than
downtown location with dark, wood paneling
and wall-to-wall windows. Views of on-site golf
course and outdoor patio. Big, open fireplace.

Date visited: ....

Went with: ....

Notes: ....

....

....

My rating: ....

Ruth's Chris Steakhouse

● ● ● ● ● ● ● ● ● ● ● ● ● ● ● ● ● ● ●

Downtown (East) Map
309 SW 3rd Ave.
(503) 221-4518
www.ruthschris.com

Happy Hours
4:00–6:00pm Daily

Food Deals 3
$3.00–$7.00
12 or so high-quality apps like seared ahi tuna,
scallops, tenderloin or prime rib sliders, burger,
BBQ shrimp, beef tenderloin brochettes.

Drink Specials 3
$3.00 drafts; $5.00 red or white wine
$5.00 martinis, cosmos and lemondrops

Atmosphere 3
Richly-appointed, dark and dimly lit, fine-dining
steakhouse. You *can* afford good steak and
a fancy evening out when you go here for their
Happy Hour. Enjoy the good life.

Date visited: _____

Went with: _____

Notes: _____

_____

_____

My rating: _____

Benson Hotel

• •

Downtown (Eaast) Map
309 SW Broadway
(503) 228-2000
www.bensonhotel.com

Happy Hours
4:00–6:00pm and 9:00–close Daily

Food Deals 3
$3.00–$8.00
Yay! Happy Hour is *back* with delicious food like
calamari, crab wontons, ham and brie crostata,
spicy garlic shrimp, truffle fries, fondue, salads,
sandwiches, cheese plate, fresh fruit medley.

Drink Specials 0
Sadly, no drink specials

Atmosphere 3
Historic and Fancy with a capital "F," their Palm
Court Bar in the hotel lobby offers the opportunity
to dine in high-style for less. Perfect place to pretend
you're Thurston or Lovey Howell. And it's haunted!

Date visited: ....

Went with: ....

Notes: ....

....

....

My rating: ....

Heathman Hotel

8

* * * * * * * * * * * * * * * * * * * *

Downtown (West) Map
1001 SW Broadway
(503) 241-4100
www.portland.heathmanhotel.com

Happy Hours
All day 2:00pm–close Daily

Food Deals 3
$2.00–$6.00
Lots of unique gourmet samplings like smoked
duck, roasted quail, oysters, paté, crab cakes,
salads, dips, cheese plate, clams, risotto, burger.
Smaller potions of regular menu = Happy Hour.

Drink Specials 1
$5.00 wines

Atmosphere 3
Two traditional upscale rooms: the quiet, romantic
Tea Court in back with giant marble fireplace, and
the well-stocked Marble Bar, very popular with
the after-work crowd. A landmark since 1927.
One of the top places to Happy Hour in town.

Date visited: _____

Went with: _____

Notes: _____

_____

_____

My rating: _____

Huber's

● ●

Downtown (East) Map
411 SW 3rd Ave.
(503) 228-5686
www.hubers.com

Happy Hours
4:00–6:30pm Daily; 9:30pm–close Daily

Food Deals 3
$1.95–$3.95
Wide variety of appetizers with a good mix of
options: turkey (sandwich, enchilada or quesadilla),
wings, calamari, burger, salad, ravioli, hummus.

Drink Specials 0
Sadly, no drink specials

Atmosphere 3
Historic architecture and design; giant domed
stained-glass ceiling; open tables and cozy
booths make it a pleasant, warm meeting place.
Watch the Spanish coffee "shows!" Portland's
oldest restaurant.

Date visited: _____

Went with: _____

Notes: _____

_____

_____

My rating: _____

74

Jake's Famous Crawfish

● ●

Downtown (West) Map
401 SW 12th Ave.
(503) 226-1419
www.jakesfamouscrawfish.com

Happy Hours
3:00–6:00pm Daily; 9:00–close Sun–Thurs
10:00pm–close Fri–Sat

Food Deals 3+
$1.95–$4.95
Some outstanding, hearty sizes! Cheeseburger
or chicken sandwich *with* fries only $2.95, fish
tacos, calamari, gumbo, sushi rolls, salmon cake.

Drink Specials 1
$5.75 Rotating nightly drink specials

Atmosphere 3
Old-school fun with traditional class; outdoor
sidewalk dining. Considered one of the top
seafood restaurants in the nation, Jake's has been
a downtown landmark for more than 110 years.

Date visited: _____

Went with: _____

Notes: _____

_____

_____

My rating: _____

Jake's Grill

●●●●●●●●●●●●●●●●●●●●●●●●●●

Downtown (West) Map
611 SW 10th Ave.
(503) 220-1850
www.jakesgrill.com

Happy Hours
3:00–6:00pm Mon–Fri; 9:30–close Mon–Thurs
10:00pm–close Fri–Sat; 3:00pm–close Sundays★

Food Deals 3+
$1.95–$4.95
Over a dozen menu items with outstanding hearty
sizes: wings, cheeseburger with fries, ahi tuna
skewers, hummus, pot stickers, BBQ chicken
pizza, pork sliders, quesadilla, ceviche, ribs.

Drink Specials 1
Tuesday $4.00 wells; Thursday $3.00 select pints

Atmosphere 3
Stately and traditional with convivial class; fancy
white jacket and bowtie servers; connected with
impressive Governor Hotel.

Date visited: _____

Went with: _____

Notes: _____

_____

_____

My rating: _____

76

McCormick & Schmick's

• •

Waterfront and Downtown (East) Maps

Portland (see page 234)
0309 SW Montgomery; (503) 220-1865
Beaverton
9945 SW Beaverton-Hillsdale Hwy.; (503) 643-1322
www.mccormickandschmicks.com
Tigard (Bridgeport Village)
17015 SW 72nd Ave.; (503) 684-5490

Happy Hours
3:00–6:00pm Daily; 9:00pm–close Daily
Hours may vary slightly with each location

Food Deals 3
$1.95–$4.95
Menu is just a bit different at each restaurant.
All are locally notorious for being a delicious value.

Drink Specials 2
Suburb locations have added drink deals!

Atmosphere 3
Classic and popular upscale restaurants.

Date visited: _____

Went with: _____

Notes: _____

_____

_____

My rating: _____

Portland City Grill

Downtown (East) Map
111 SW Fifth Ave., 30th Floor
(503) 450-0030
www.portlandcitygrill.com

Happy Hours
4:30–6:30pm Mon–Sat; 4:00pm–close Sunday★
10:00pm–mid Mon–Thur; 10:00pm–1:00am Fri-Sat

Food Deals 3+
$1.95–$4.95
One of the best and biggest menus in town!
blackened tuna, soba noodle salad, burger, ahi,
tenderloin or chicken satay, salads, and more.

Drink Specials 0
Sadly, no drink specials

Atmosphere 3
Way higher than just a "3" for atmosphere on
a clear day! Portland's highest building hosts
one of our best Happy Hours, and is perfect
for out-of-town guests. Get there early and try
to get a window table. Sunset on Sundays!

Date visited: _____

Went with: _____

Notes: _____

_____

_____

My rating: _____

Stanford's

●●●●●●●●●●●●●●●●●●●●●

9

Waterfront and Lloyd Center Maps

<u>Portland</u>
913 Lloyd Center; (503) 335-0811
1440 N. Jantzen Beach Center; (503) 285-2005
<u>Hillsboro</u>
2770 NW 188th Ave.; (503) 645-8000
<u>Lake Oswego</u>
14801 Kruse Oaks Dr.; (503) 620-3541
www.stanfords.com

Happy Hours
3:00–6:00pm Daily; 9:00pm–close Daily
Hours vary slightly per location

Food Deals 3
$2.00-$4.00
Delicious menu is just a bit different at each
restaurant. All are apreciated by many a fan.

Drink Specials 2
Most have drink specials now!
Usually $3.50 microbrews, wine and wells

Atmosphere 3
Classic and popular upscale restaurants with
the Happy Hour action at the central bar.

Date visited: _____

Went with: _____

Notes: _____

_____

_____

My rating: _____

Uptown Billiards Club

NW/Nob Hill Map
120 NW 23rd Ave .
(503) 226-6909
www.uptownbilliards.com

Happy Hours
4:00–6:00pm Tues–Sat

TOP TEN FAVORITE!

Food Deals 3+
$10.00 (only for parties of 2–8) FIVE-course fine-dining experience! Menu rotates every two weeks and typically highlights a super fresh seasonal ingredient (i.e. tomatoes or apples) which is then used in every course served. Phenomenal!

Drink Specials 3
$10.00 flight of wine; tastings are paired with each course to complement food perfectly.

Atmosphere 3
Also totally different in the pool hall classification with its upscale class and elegance. Fancy, tucked-away billiards room. Non-smoking. <u>Must RSVP</u>! Check website for menu of the week.

Date visited: _____
Went with: _____
Notes: _____
_____
_____

My rating: _____

Wilfs

● ●

★7

Pearl (off map)
800 NW 6th Avenue (Union Station)
(503) 223-0070
www.wilfsrestaurant.com

Happy Hours
6:00–7:30pm Tues–Sat

Food Deals 3
$3.50–$6.00
Half-off limited seasonal bar menu items like
french onion soup, Caesar salad, white bean
herb dip, salad, butternut squash pizza or bread
pudding.

Drink Specials 0
Sadly, no drink specials

Atmosphere 3
A beautiful, top-notch Portland classic that falls
off the radar, but just started a Happy Hour!
Enjoy a fancy evening out and enjoy their classy
jazz lounge, then stay for some live music
(check calendar).

Date visited: _____

Went with: _____

Notes: _____

_____

_____

My rating: _____

Branch Whiskey Bar

Alberta Map 2926 NE Alberta; 206-6266

Happy Hours 5:00–7:00pm/10:00–close Daily

Food Deals 2 $2.00 off unique but limited menu with items like white bean puree, pork rillet, salad, burger.

Drink Specials 3 $3.00 drafts; $1.50 PBRs; $5.00 wines; $3.00 wells

Atmosphere 2 Get your whiskey on or branch out to scotch or rye at this small and cozy, brick-walled bar, that's really more of a restaurant, ambiance-wise.

Bistro 921 www.bistro-921.com

Downtown Map 921 SW 6th Ave; (503) 220-2185

Happy Hours 3:30-6:00pm & 9:00-10:00pm Mon–Fri

Food Deals 2 $3.00–$6.00 Soups, sliders, salads, smothered tots, shrimp, spinach dip, quesadilla.

Drink Specials 0 Sadly, no drink specials

Atmosphere 2 Located in the Hilton near the Schnitz. Happy Hour in the Bistro Bar only. Enter through the glamorous lobby and restaurant.

Delta Café www.deltacafebar.com

SE (Not on Map) 4607 SE Woodstock; (503) 771-3101

Happy Hours 4:00–6:00pm/11:00pm-1:00am Mon–Thur
★All night Tuesday includes $5.00 specialty cocktails

Food Deals 3 $1.00–$3.00 Hush puppies, sweet potato fries, corn bread, fritters, mac & cheese

Drink Specials 2 $2.50 drafts or wells, $5.00 wine

Atmosphere 2 They've decked themselves out with very colorful SE PDX-meets-Delta style! Loud, garish and fun with graffiti and folk art everywhere. Cash only.

Echo www.echorestaurant.com

North/NE Map 2225 NE MLK Blvd.; (503) 460-3246

Happy Hours 4:30–6:00pm Mon–Fri;
3:00–6:00pm Sat–Sun

Food Deals 2 $4.00–$6.00 Fresh comfort food plus:
salads, portobello sandwich, hummus, burger, pizza,
mac & cheese, stuffed peppers, crab and cheese dip.

Drink Specials 1 Some 10:00pm drink specials;
$10.00 off every bottle of wine Sunday nights

Atmosphere 2 A welcoming casual haunt; brick
warehouse effect softened by towering orange
draperies and original art.

Elephant's Deli www.elephantsdeli.com

NW/Nob Hill Map 115 NW 22nd Ave.; (503) 299-6304

Happy Hours 5:00–7:00 Mon–Sat

Food Deals 2 $3.95 Nice little array of eats like
pizza, fondue, aardvark chicken strips, mahi mahi
(plus a whole "Whole Foods"-like deli).

Drink Specials 2 $3.00 beer, $4 wine, $5 cocktails

Atmosphere 2 It's a cute little, urban bar in an quaint,
new country store. Eat and shop, drink and bring home
good wine, *and* grab gourmet to go! Outdoor deck too.

Hilt www.thehiltbar.com

Alberta Map 1934 NE Alberta St; (971) 255-1793

Happy Hours 4:00-7:00pm Daily; ★Sunday 'til 2:30am

Food Deals 2 $2.00–$4.00 Half-off appetizers
which are kind of bar-ish and kinda Mediterranean.

Drink Specials 2 $1.00 off taps & wells
Atmosphere 2 Not decorated crazily to the hilt, and
actually quite non-descript, but a comfortable neighborhood hangout on Alberta with big outdoor patio.

Kenny & Zuke's www.kennyandzukes.com

Downtown Map 1038 SW Stark; (503) 222-DELI

Happy Hours 4:00–6:00pm Mon–Fri

Food Deals 2 $2.75–$7.75 Just a bit of a price break on a few random, rockin' sandwiches like reuben sliders, pastrami (praise the pastrami!), burgers, bagel & lox.

Drink Specials 1 $2.50 draft beers

Atmosphere 2 A real New York deli in Portland! With a twist of being fresh and clean, bright and upbeat, retro and modern at once, it's a big, happy space.

Melt www.meltportland.com

NW/Nob Hill Map 716 NW 21st; (503) 295-4944

Happy Hours 4:00–6:00pm / 9:00–close Mon–Sat

Food Deals 3 $3.00–$5.00 This place has the best sandwiches! Big deals on lots: mini-melts w/fries, salads, fritters, crab dip, soup, mushroom bruschetta.

Drink Specials 3 $3 drafts, $4 wines, $5 cocktails

Atmosphere 2 Small, simple, natural and artsy bar/café. Multi-colored, hanging lamps and colorful, original paintings add a touch of funk. Open-to-street, over-sized windows and sidewalk tables make it social.

West Café www.westcafepdx.com

Downtown Map 1201 SW Jefferson; (503) 227-8189

Happy Hours 4:30-7:00pm & 9:00pm-close Mon-Sat

Food Deals 2 $1.00 off *very* extensive menu of fresh, gourmet and unique items (snacks, soups, salads).

Drink Specials 1 $1.00 off beer and wine

Atmosphere 2 They do lunch, dinner and brunch and fit somewhere between being a nice restaurant and cozy café. Elegant touches mix with diner styles and it works. Occasional "recession" or "bail out" deals.

Beervana

Microbreweries
Brewpubs
Great Beer

Full-page Reviews
The best Happy Hours at the biggest breweries
are detailed on their own page. Admire those
giant copper tanks that brew your beer right in
front of you at any of these impressive micro-
breweries. Have guests in town visiting? Take
'em around on a micro tour to sample our
famous NW brews. They are so goooood!

Half-Pint Reviews
The "Half-Pint" reviews are Happy Hours with
less impressive Happy Hour deals and/or
ambiance, but have delicious beer nonetheless.
This whole chapter needs to be a book in itself!

Other Listings
Don't miss out on the many places that make
it a priority to offer an array of tasty taps!

B.J.'s Brewhouse

●●●●●●●●●●●●●●●●●●●●●●●●●●●

8

Waterfront Map
12105 N. Center
(503) 289-5566
www.bjsrestaurants.com

Happy Hours
3:00–7:00pm Mon–Fri
10:00–11:00pm Sun–Thur

Food Deals 2
$2.00 off appetizers (17 items)
1/2 price personal pizzas
Huge lineup of all the bar basics including wings,
nachos, potato skins, spring rolls, fries, chips
and salsa, lettuce wraps, eggrolls, and sliders.

Drink Specials 2
$1.00 off pints and wells

Atmosphere 3
Warm and friendly pub with golden beer-colored
walls, red brick, big ol' beer vats and a long bar.
Doesn't quite hit typical top marks for style, but
for the area and what it is, it's nice.

Date visited: _____

Went with: _____

Notes: _____

_____

_____

My rating: _____

Bridgeport Brewpub

Pearl Map
1313 NW Marshall
(503) 241-3612
www.bridgeportbrewandalehouse.com

Happy Hours
4:00–6:00pm Mon–Fri
10:00pm–close Tues–Sat (food and beer only)

Food Deals 3
$2.50–$6.00
Cheeseburgers, pulled pork sandwiches, Caesar,
spinach artichoke dip, chips and salsa, nachos,
hummus, skewers, wings, mussels, pizzas.

Drink Specials 2
$2.75 pints; $4.00 bartender's choice cocktail

Atmosphere 3
Slick and new new, big-city-style brewery,
bakery and coffee shop in renovated loft building;
cavernous open area with the brick, iron and
wood basics; outdoor seating.

Date visited: _____

Went with: _____

Notes: _____

_____

_____

My rating: _____

Deschute's Brewery

7

Pearl Map
210 NW 11th Ave.
(503) 296-4906
www.deschutesbrewery.com

Happy Hours
4:00–6:00pm Mon–Fri

Food Deals 2
$2.95–$4.95
Mini-meals made with beer or made to go with it:
BBQ short ribs, pork sliders, penne pasta, fries,
Caesar salad, pretzels, French onion soup, pizza.

Drink Specials 1
$3.50 beer-of-the-day (20oz.)

Atmosphere 3
A "don't miss" for beer lovin' visitors from out of
town (locals love it too, and it consistently draws
a big crowd). Huge, cavernous interior captures
the spirits of the Pacific Northwest, complete with
bear totem poles, exposed brick, and lots of wood.

Date visited: _____

Went with: _____

Notes: _____

_____

_____

My rating: _____

Henry's Tavern

Pearl Map
10 NW 12th Ave.
(503) 227-5320
www.henrystavern.com

Happy Hours
3:00–6:00pm Daily; 9:00pm–close Sun–Wed
10:30pm–midnight Fri–Sat

Food Deals 3
$2.00–$5.00
BBQ chicken pizza, Caesar, mac & cheese, soup,
sushi roll, cheeseburger, killer Gorgonzola fries,
crabcakes and orange chicken, to name a few.

Drink Specials 0

Atmosphere 3
A long-time Portland favorite; warm, but spacious
ex-brewery; open two-story seating; huge center
bar; loft-style bricks & iron; patio (not available for
HH seating). More than 100 beers on tap with
refrigerated bar top to keep beers nice & cold.

Date visited: _____

Went with: _____

Notes: _____

_____

_____

My rating: _____

Hopworks Urban Brewery

• •

Southeast Map
2944 SE Powell Blvd
(503) 232-4677
www.hopworksbeer.com

Happy Hours
3:00–6:00pm & 9:00pm–close Daily
(Fri & Sat 10:00pm–midnight)

Food Deals 2
$2.25–$4.75
Food to most perfectly complement their perfect beer: pizza, pretzels, peanuts, sausages, fries, wings, soup, hummus, and salads.

Drink Specials 1
Beer is 75 cents off

Atmosphere 3
Eco-brewpub with organic beer, fresh local ingredients, and a sustainable building. Very cool bike "rack" over bar. Bike-, banquet-, baby- and beer-garden-friendly. Commonly referred to as HUB.

Date visited: _____

Went with: _____

Notes: _____

_____

_____

My rating: _____

McTarnahan's

NW/Nob Hill Map
2730 NW 31st Ave.
(503) 228-5269
www.macsbeer.com

Happy Hours
3:00–6:00pm & 9:00pm–close Mon–Sat

Food Deals 2
$1.95–$3.95
Simple menu of bar eats like pizza, tacos, burger,
Caesar salad, hummus, garlic fries, or sliders.

Drink Specials 2
$3.30 drafts; $3.95 wines or mimosa

Atmosphere 3
A little bit of everything strewn throughout 3-4
rooms, with the patio being a highlight. The back
restaurant room is more cozy and pubby than
the front bar, which has views of hi-def TVs and
the giant copper beer vats. Across from Boedecker
Cellars for a quick weekend wine tasting first.

Date visited: ....

Went with: ....

Notes: ....

....

....

My rating: ....

Rock Bottom

Downtown (East) Map
206 SW Morrison
(503) 796-2739
www.rockbottom.com

Happy Hours
2:00–6:00pm Mon–Fri; 9:00pm–close Sun–Thurs
11:00pm–close Fri & Sat

Food Deals 3
$1.95–$3.95
12 tasty appetizers like pork, chicken or beef
sliders, chips & guacamole, wings, spinach dip,
hummus, nachos, mac & cheese, burgers,
chicken enchiladas, chicken Caesar, ceviche.

Drink Specials 1
$1.00 off pints (early)

Atmosphere 3
Corporate-style open brewery; warm coppers
mixed with wood under soaring lofted ceilings;
bustling big bar area; sidewalk dining.

Date visited: _____

Went with: _____

Notes: _____

_____

_____

My rating: _____

Half-Pint Reviews

●●●●●●●●●●●●●●●●●●●●●●●●●●●●●

Alameda Brew House
4765 NE Fremont; (503) 460-9025
www.alamedabrewhouse.com
*Beers are produced on location; hand-crafted ales
and freshly prepared food.*
Happy Hour: 3:00–6:00pm Mon-Fri; 9:00pm–close Sat
Beer special: $3.00 pints; $3.95 wines
Food specials: $4.00 appetizers (good food!)

Amnesia Brewing
832 N. Beech; (503) 281-7708
Happy Hour: 4:00–6:00pm Mon-Fri
Beer special: $3.00 pints
Food specials: None (but cheap grub)
*Brewpub in the eclectic Mississippi neighborhood;
alluring front patio hang-out; beer afficionados love it.*

Bridgeport Ale House
3632 SE Hawthorne; (503) 233-6540
www.bridgeportbrewandalehouse.com
Happy Hour: 3:00–6:00pm Daily
Beer special: $2.75 pints
Food specials: $2.50–$5.00 ($8.00 pizzas)
Menu changes seasonally.
*A smaller, neighborhood off-shoot of downtown s
Bridgeport Brewpub with open windows to street*

Green Dragon
928 SE 9th Ave.; (503) 517-0606
pdxgreendragon.com
Happy Hour: 4:00–6:00pm Daily
Beer special: No drink discounts
Food specials: $3.00–$5.00 Fresh, tasty and varied
bar eats like pork sliders, brat bites, fish & chips
*Open garage-style brewery with a utopian beer
selection of 19 perfectly selected rotating taps.
Nice big beer garden next to the Q-hut.*

Laurelwood Brewpubs

1728 NE 40thAve.; (503) 335-9084
5115 NE Sandy; (503) 282-0622
www.laurelwoodbrewpub.com
Happy Hour varies per location; Closed Mondays

Laurelwood/NW

2327 NW Kearney; (503) 228-5553
<u>Happy Hour:</u> 3:00–6:00pm Daily; 9:00–10:00pm
Sun–Thurs; 10:00–11:00pm Fri–Sat
<u>Beer special:</u> $1.00 off pints ($3.00)
<u>Food specials:</u> $4.00 Beef or veggie burgers, happy
nachos, garlic fries, fish tacos, hummus, salad.
Cozy restaurant in big, old Victorian house with converted rooms that make it feel like home. Outdoor seating on two porches; head upstairs for family fun.

Lompocs www.newoldlompoc.com

Hedgehouse 3412 SE Division; (503) 235-2215
$3.25 pints 4:00–6:00pm Daily & All Sat–Sun
$2.50 pints Tues

Lompoc Fifth Quadrant & Sidebar Weekends
3901 N. Williams; (503) 288-3996
<u>Happy Hour:</u> 4:00–6:00pm M-F; 11:00am–close S-S
<u>Beer special:</u> 2.50 pints all day Tuesday; $3.25 beers
other Happy Hours; $3.00 Bloody Mary Sunday
<u>Food specials:</u> Half-off apps
Fresh and colorful, loft-style brewpub; long wooden booths for socializing; outdoor patio open to restaurant.

New Old Lompoc See review on page 255.
1616 NW 23rd Ave.; (503) 225-1855

Oaks Bottom Pub 1621 SE Bybee; (503) 459-4988
<u>Happy Hour:</u> 3:00–6:00pm Daily
10:00pm–close Sun–Thurs ($2.00 beer/no food)
<u>Beer special:</u> $3.25 Lompoc pints; $1.00 off wells
<u>Food specials:</u> $4.00 It's all about the "totchos"
(tater tot nachos), pita-zza hummus platter; beer brat
snausages. No food discounts on weekends.
Small but popular neighborhood haunt with a café appeal and outside seating on back patio.

Lucky Lab Brewing Company

915 SE Hawthorne; (503) 236-3555
1945 NW Quimby; (503) 517-4352
7675 SW Capitol Hwy.; (503) 244-2537
New? Potential plans for old Roux space in mid-2010.
www.luckylab.com
Happy Hour: Miser Mondays at the Hawthorne
Brewpub and Tightwad Tuesdays at Capitol Hwy.
Decent and well-priced food, but no special HH deal.
*Casual favorites in big woody spaces. Big rooms,
dog and family-friendly. Places that just feel right.*

Mashtun Brewpub

2204 NE Alberta; (503) 548-4491
Happy Hour: 4:00–6:00pm Mon–Fri
Beer special: $1.00 off house beers; $1.00 off wells
Food specials: $2.50–$6.00 Tasty basics that go
well with beer and pool. Generous servings of tots!
*Very casual and warehouse-y pub with big patio too.
Large and open garage-like space with free pool,
darts and jukebox. Big game tables.*

Raccoon Lodge & Brew Pub

7424 SW Beaverton-Hillsdale Hwy.; (503) 296-0110
www.raclodge.com
Happy Hour: 3:00–6:00pm / 9:00pm–close Mon–Fri
(4:00–6:00pm and all day Sat–Sun in the Den
Beer special: $3.50 three select microbrews 20 oz.
Food specials: $3.00–$7.00 big bar menu
Simple and clean, basic pub with pool and TV.

Rogue Ales Public House

1339 NW Flanders; (503) 222-5910
www.rogue.com
Happy Hour: 3:00–5:00pm Mon–Fri (food only)
Food specials: $3.00–$5.00 bar food basics
*A fun and rouge-ish interior with several bawdy bar
rooms befitting the name and attitude.*

Roots Organic Brewing

1520 SE 7th Ave.; (503) 235-7668
www.rootsorganicbrewing.com
Happy Hour: 4:00–6:00pm Wed–Fri; All Tuesday
Beer special: $3.25 pints ($2.50 all Tuesdays)
Food specials: $2.50–$6.50 9-10 bar menu items
*Oregon s first (and only) all-organic brewery. Very
casual hang-out with natural and simple decor.*

Salmon Creek Brewery

108 W Evergreen, Vancouver; (360) 993-1827
Happy Hour: 3:00–6:00pm Mon–Thurs; 4:00–6:00pm Sat
Beer special: $3.50 pints
Food specials: $2.50–$4.50 pub munchies
Outstanding beer garden and hand-crafted beer.

Tugboat Brewing Co.

711 SW Ankeny; (503) 226-2508
Happy Hour: 4:00–7:00pm Mon–Fri
Beer special: $1.00 off drafts
Downtown Portland's oldest microbrewery.

Widmer Gasthaus

929 N Russell; (503) 281-3333
www.widmer.com
Happy Hour: 11:00am–5:00pm Sun; 2:00–10:00pm Mon;
2:00–5:00pm Tues–Fri
Beer special: $1.00 off pints
Food specials: $1.50–$6.95 Bar menu w/ sandwiches
$5.00 cheesebugers Sun–Mon
*Fun party space with bricks and beer-colored walls.
Free tours Fridays and Saturdays (book ahead).*

Also see Full Sail Brewery's Outpost (**McCormick & Schmick
Harborside Pilsner Room**) in the Waterfront Section,
p. 235.

Bailey's Tap Room www.baileystaproom.com
213 SW Broadway; (503) 295-1004
20 Rotating Taps of Craft Ales and Lagers.

Belmont Station www.belmont-station.com
4500 SE Stark; (503) 232-8538
1,000 beers in the store; café next door to drink & dine.
<u>Happy Hour:</u> $3.00 Special Beer-of-the-day

By the Bottle www.www.bottledbrews.com
104 W. Evergreen, Vancouver, WA (360) 696-0012
A store, a sight to see. Over 600 types of beer!

Concordia Ale House
3276 NE Killingsworth; (503) 287-3929
Simple inside, but exquisite beer lists (150+ bottles).
<u>Happy Hour:</u> 3:00–6:00pm Daily $1.50 Old Germans

Dublin Pub www.dublinpubpdx.com
6821 SW Beaverton-Hillside Hwy.; (503) 297-2889
59 beers on tap; over 50 more in bottles. Yes!
<u>Happy Hour:</u> 3:00–7:00pm Daily (5:00-7:00pm Sun)
Drink special: $3.00 microbrews, $3 wells; $4 wines

Hop & Vine www.thehopandvine.com
1914 N. Killingsworth; (503) 954-3322
Cozy space with full bar and retail space too.
<u>Happy Hour:</u> 3:00–6:00pm Daily $1.00 off beer & wine

Horsebrass Pub www.horsebrass.com
4534 SE Belmont; (503) 232-2202
Legendary English Pub style and has over 50 taps!

Produce Row Cafe www.producerowcafe.com
204 SE Oak; (503) 232-8355
27 well-chosen taps and over 200 bottled beers.
<u>Happy Hour:</u> 4:00–7:00pm Mon–Sat $1.00 off drafts

Prost! www.prostportland.com
4237 N. Mississippi; (503) 954-2684
Nice German pub w/over-sized beer mugs and boots!

Saraveza www.saraveza.com
1004 N Killingsworth; (503) 206-4252;
200+ bottles and 10 rotating taps!
<u>Happy Hour:</u> 3:30-5:30pm Wed-Mon $1.50 1/2 pours

McMenamins

They're everywhere!
Hotels, movies, live bands, pubs
(53 properties and counting)

www.mcmenamins.com
On-site brewing at many brewpubs

Giant kudos and cheers!
OK, so I'm breaking out of the box a bit now
to give this group of restaurants special focus. I
am a *huge* fan of the McMenamins establish-
ments! I especially love their hotel properties,
which are some not-to-be-missed Portland expe-
riences. They really know how to pull together
unique spaces loaded with personality! There's
always lots to look at and they pick some very
interesting and creative themes. Happy-Hour-
wise, they're only average, but their menu has
lots of cheap eats, so just go any time. Most
places have small discounts on food and beer
4:00–6:00pm weekdays. Also note that you can
drink beer and eat inside the movie theaters!
Although this is a Portland city-focused book,
I've included info on some of their stellar places
outside of Portland city limits as well. Their hotels
are great places to stay for a fun weekend away!

Hotels and several of their 50+ bars are listed
on the following pages. Make it a mission to hit
them all!

McMenamins Hotels

Edgefield
2126 SW Halsey; Troutdale
(503) 669-8610
38-acre renovated "Poor Farm;" golf course, movie
theater, beer garden, casual and fine-dining, wine
bar, Jerry Garcia bar, Little Red Shed Pub, and Spa.

The Grand Lodge
3505 Pacific Ave.; Forest Grove
(503) 992-9533
Stately but fun ex-Masonic lodge and nursing home;
multiple restaurants; cozy, small bars, movies, giant
soaking tub, and frisbee golf. Good positioning for
touring Wine Country!

Hotel Oregon
310 NE Evans Street; McMinnville; (503) 472-8427
Weekend get-away in wine country; rooftop bar
(great for viewing UFOs), pub, back bar, Cellar Bar,
pool/billiards.

Kennedy School
5736 NE 33rd Ave.; Portland; (503) 249-3983
Detention Bar, Honors Bar, Boiler Room Bar, movies,
soaking pool, outdoor courtyard beer garden, party/
meeting rooms, restaurant.

Old St. Francis School
700 NW Bond; Bend
(541) 382-5174
Old 1936 Catholic schoolhouse transformed into
a heavenly entertainment complex.

White Eagle
836 N. Russell; Portland (503) 335-8900
A small "rock 'n' roll hotel" with resident "spirits"
(it's reportedly haunted), nightly bands, saloon,
and outdoor seasonal beer garden.

McMenamins Pubs

Select favorites – see their website for all pubs.

Bagdad Theater/Greater Trumps
3702 SE Hawthorne; (503) 236-9234
Arabian Nights inspired movie theater and secret pub.

Blue Moon Tavern
432 NW 21st Ave.; (503) 223-3184
Meandering bar with table-top fireplace in the round
and pool tables; outdoor sidewalk seating.

Chapel Pub
430 N Killingsworth; (503) 286-0372
A sanctuary with lots of cozy rooms. Outdoor patio.

Crystal Ballroom
1332 W Burnside; (503) 225-0047
Awesome place to see concerts! The ballroom floor
is spring-loaded so it bounces slightly, and there's
'80s nights downstairs at Lola's.

McMenamins on the Columbia
1801 SE Columbia River Dr.
Vancouver, WA; (360) 699-1521
Beautiful riverside view of the Columbia

McMenamins Tavern & Pool
1716 NW 23rd Ave.; (503) 227-0929
Heated outdoor tables; big pool room.

Mission Theater
1624 NW Glisan; (503) 223-4527
$3.00 movies in old Swedish evangelical mission.

Ram's Head
2282 NW Hoyt; (503) 221-0098
Sophisticated manly-man haven.

Ringler's Pub
1332 W. Burnside; (503) 225-0627
Funky ex-auto garage.

Crystal Hotel scheduled to open mid-2010!

Cocktails & Wine

For Girls' Night Out
–or–
Make it a Date

The following pages list upscale cocktail lounges and wine bars that offer perfect environments for sitting back with a good drink and getting discounts on food at Happy Hour to boot. Start girls' night out early and hop around a bit. Meet a date out for a pre-dinner or after-show drink. Take your girlfriend somewhere nice. Or just saddle up to the bar and watch the barmasters do their thing!

820/Mint

820 N Russell
(503) 284-5518
www.mintrestaurant.com

Happy Hours
4:00–8:00pm Mon–Tues★; 4:00pm–close Wed★
4:00–6:30pm Thurs–Sat; 4:00pm–close Sun★

Food Deals 2
$2.50–$6.00
It's all about the sweet potato fries! Limited but
delicious, unique menu: lamb burger, calamari,
soup, and salad.

Drink Specials 3
$3.50 well drinks; $2.75 draft beers
$5.00 selected cocktails (yum!)

Atmosphere 3
Connected to gorgeous and hip Mint Restaurant
(where you can Happy Hour 5-6:30pm); 820 is a
trendy, upscale ultra-lounge with nice back deck
area to most pleasantly enjoy on a nice day.

Date visited:

Went with:

Notes:

My rating:

Alu Wine Bar

NE/ Map
2831 NE ML King Jr. Blvd.
(503) 262-9463
www.aluwinebar.com

Happy Hours
5:00–6:30pm Mon–Sat

Food Deals 2
$4.00–$6.00
Evolving menu of food that pairs well with wine,
like cheese and charcuterie plates, olives, breads.
Don't miss their flavored popcorn of the day! ($1.00)

Drink Specials 3
$2.00 select bottled beer; $5.00 wine selection
$2.00 off specialty cocktails

Atmosphere 3
Gorgeous decor! Great back patio! It's striking,
memorable, gorgeous and luscious – a total
favorite! Funky, oversized door entrance to dark,
brick-walled party room with lush, upholstered
sofas and chairs with more upstairs with bar.

Date visited: _____

Went with: _____

Notes: _____

_____

_____

My rating: _____

Bar Avignon

8

SE Map
2138 SE Division
(503) 517-0808
www.baravignon.com

Happy Hours
4:00–6:00pm Mon–Fri

Food Deals 2
$3.00–$6.00
Ultra-fresh and gourmet small menu of fancy items like prosciutto wrapped greens, smoked salmon, mussels, baguettes, marinated olives.

Drink Specials 3
$3.50 drafts (nice choices); $5.00 wines
$4.50 wells; $5.00 select cocktail

Atmosphere 2
Small, industrial-fresh restaurant with big bar and small, back table room surrounded by wine. Lots of light by day makes it coffee-shop-like, but by night it's more romantic, but not Frenchy like the name might imply.

Date visited: _____

Went with: _____

Notes: _____

_____

_____

My rating: _____

Bartini

NW/Nob Hill Map
2108 NW Glisan
(503) 224-7919
www.urbanfondue.com

Happy Hours
4:00–6:30pm Tues–Sat
9:30pm–close Tues–Thur
4:00pm–close Sunday and Monday★

Food Deals 3
$3.00–$7.00
Lots of gourmet choices, including fondue, ahi tuna sliders, crab cakes, coconut shrimp, salads, hummus, satay, skewers, flatbreads, burgers.

Drink Specials 3
Half-off teee meny martunis! Like a million of 'em!

Atmosphere 3
Black, black and more black; small & intimate martini lounge; best appreciated after sunset.

Date visited:
Went with:
Notes:

My rating:

Beaker & Flask

SE Map
727 SE Washington
(503) 235-8180
www.beakerandflask.com

Happy Hours
Drinks: 5:00–6:00pm; Food:10:00pm–close Daily

Food Deals 2
$4.00-$8.00
Choose from 3-5 items from the late-night bar menu which changes monthly to reflect the season. Unique, old-fashioned nouveau food.

Drink Specials 2
$1.00 off pints; $5.00 select specialty cocktails

Atmosphere 3
Manly-chic loft *style* with cement, blackboard, and green walls. Trendy yet simple with bar, banquette or barrel table seating. Take note of the address as it's located in an off-the-beaten path industrial park and building. Coolest at night!

Date visited: _____

Went with: _____

Notes: _____

_____

_____

My rating: _____

Gilt Club

TOP TEN FAVORITE!

Downtown (West) Map
306 NW Broadway
(503) 222-4458
www.giltclub.com

Happy Hours
5:00–6:30pm Mon–Fri

Food Deals 3
$1.00–$5.00
Delicious upscale offerings like mixed olives
or nuts, fries, salads, burger, fritter, or pizza.

Drink Specials 3
$2.50 Stellas; $5.00 wine
$5.00 appletini or Moscow mule

Atmosphere 3
Yes, it IS most luscious! Plushness abounds
with deep red walls and velvet drapes with gold
touches & sexy curves galore. WAY swanky!
Very creative touches and overall surroundings.

Date visited: _____
Went with: _____
Notes: _____
_____
_____

My rating: _____

Jo-Bar

715 NW 23rd Ave.
(503) 222-0048
www.papahaydn.com/r/6/Jo-Bar

Happy Hours
3:00–6:00pm Daily; also last hour before closing

Food Deals 2
$3.00–$8.00
French onion soup, three styles of pizza, fries, Jo Burger, homemade sweet potato chips, Cobb salad, and baked mac & cheese.

Drink Specials 3
$4.00 beer; $4.00 wine; $5.50 Daily cocktail

Atmosphere 3
Deep red and olive walls, stunning entry flower display, original art, huge iron chandelier, open stone wood oven and rotisserie, full front windows, outdoor sidewalk seating. Casually chill, yet nice.

Date visited: _____
Went with: _____
Notes: _____
....
....

My rating: _____

Metrovino

Pearl Map
1139 NW 11th Ave
(503) 517-7778
www.metrovinopdx.com

Happy Hours
4:00–6:00pm Mon–Fri

Food Deals 2
$1.00–$9.00
Delicious and seasonally fresh NW, but on the pricey side (quality costs): soups, stews and salads, cheeseburger, Hawaiian ribs or yellowtail.

Drink Specials 2
$5.00 select red, white or bubbles
$5.00 cocktails (like a midtown or metro spritz)

Atmosphere 3
Metrovino is a wonderfullly welcomed new Pearl place that could be listed as an American/NW restaurant or in the "cool & contemporary" section. But they have 80 wines by the glass or taste, so go for the vino part! And the food. Food too!

Date visited: _____

Went with: _____

Notes: _____

_____

_____

My rating: _____

Moloko Plus

North/NE Map
3967 N Mississippi
(503) 288-6272
http://www.myspace.com/molokopdx

Happy Hours
4:00–8:00pm Daily

Food Deals 2
$1.00–$5.00
Simple, light fare includes turkey, salami or chevre sandwiches, hummus, pineapple salsa and chips, tossed green salad, nut mix and other snacks.

Drink Specials 3
$1.00 and $2.00 beers; $5.00–$6.50 wines
$3.50 well drinks, $5.00 mimosas

Atmosphere 3
A secret Mississippi gem with neon symbols as signage. Ultra-retro, white and mod interior, with 60's seating in both vinyl upholstered and plasticform lounge chairs. Charming garden gazebo back deck area. They make their own infusions.

Date visited: _____

Went with: _____

Notes: _____

_____

_____

My rating: _____

Noble Rot

● ●

Lloyd Center-ish Map
1111 E Burnside
(503) 233-1999
www.noblerotpdx.com

Happy Hours
5:00–6:00pm

Food Deals 3
$2.00–$8.00
Ranges from nibblets to comfort food and changes
with the season: olives, onion rings, French fries,
cheese plate, paninos, mac & cheese, hamburger.

Drink Specials 3
$3.50 draft beer; $3.50 red or white wine
$5.50 selection of bartender's specialties

Atmosphere 3
Stunning wall-to-wall, floor-to-ceiling windows
perched high for a wide-open city view; ultra-cool
contemporary-retro interior (though toned-down
compared to prior Rocket interior); illuminated
circular glass art on ceiling. Rooftop outdoor deck!

Date visited: ....

Went with: ....

Notes: ....

....

....

My rating: ....

NV / Eclectic

9

Downtown Map
204 SW Yamhill
(503) 200-5500
www.myspace.com/envyloungepdx

Happy Hours
3:00–7:00pm Tues–Fri

Food Deals 3
$3.00–$5.00
Big and cheap menu with wide mix: soup, salad, fries, rings, steak bites, burger, satay, skewers, quesadillas, calamari, bacon mac, pizza.

Drink Specials 3
$3.00 drafts; $4.00 wells; $2.00 off cocktails
1/2 off bottles of wine Thursdays

Atmosphere 3
Extremely cool, multi-room space that takes the old H_2O decor up a level with several very striking party lounges. Clubby, but quiet early on. Several seating and lounging areas make it great for groups. Don't be turned off by their "website".

Date visited: ....

Went with: ....

Notes: ....

....

....

My rating: ....

The Observatory

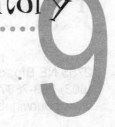

Southeast (Off Map)
8115 SE Stark
(503) 445-6284
www.theobservatorypdx.com

Happy Hours
3:00–6:00pm Daily; 10:00pm–mid Tues–Thur

Food Deals 3
$2.00–$5.00
Extra points for being a foodie place, but limited choices at HH. Seasonal: salad, soup, smoked whitefish spread, ginger sake mussels.

Drink Specials 3
$1.00 domestics (cans); $3.00 microbrews
$5.00 house wines; $3.00 wells; $5.00 cocktail

Atmosphere 2
Not too lounge-y, and it's probably more of a restaurant, but their signature cocktails are quite impressive! Big L-shaped bar dominates this upscale diner beneath high-strung globe light constellation.

Date visited: _____

Went with: _____

Notes: _____

_____

_____

My rating: _____

Pour Wine Bar

2755 NE Broadway
(503) 288-7687
www.pourwinebar.com

Happy Hours
4:30–6:30pm Mon–Sat

Food Deals 2
$2.00
Very good, but only discounted options are
cheese panini, marinated olives, and roasted
hazelnuts. Regular menu has some cheapies too.

Drink Specials 3
$3.00 pours of select red and white wines
$5.00 off select bottles; $15.00 flights
$2.00 Stellas

Atmosphere 3
Striking 1960's-style Space Odyssey lounge;
cool white retro chairs and walls; string art
mural; silver and real flower touches.

Date visited: _____

Went with: _____

Notes: _____

_____

_____

My rating: _____

Sapphire Hotel

5008 SE Hawthorne
(503) 232-6333
www.thesapphirehotel.com

Happy Hours
4:00pm–6:00pm Mon–Fri
10:00pm-close Sun–Thurs
2:00–6:00pm Sat–Sun

Food Deals 3
$3.00–$6.00
Meze platters, soup, several salads, artichoke
dip, blackened chicken, seasonal crostini.

Drink Specials 2
$2.00 PBRs; $4.00 selected wine
$4.00 well drinks; $5.00 nightly drink special

Atmosphere 3
Mysteriously sexy and intriguing; trés swanky!
Intimate creative lounge decor. Ex-brothel.
Outdoor sidewalk seating.

Date visited: _____
Went with: _____
Notes: _____
_____
_____

My rating: _____

Shaken Martini Lounge

4605 NE Fremont
(503)282-4007

Happy Hours
4:00pm–6:30pm and 9:30pm–close Mon–Fri

Food Deals 3
$1.00–$3.00
Half-off flavored flatbreads, spinach salad, soup and baked brie plate. Best grilled sandwiches (ever!) from regular menu only $6.00.

Drink Specials 3+
$2.00 drafts; $4.00 wine; $4.00 martinis

Atmosphere 3
Big living room style lounge with several seating areas. Brings the outside in and the inside out with a connected, peaceful and pleasant patio. James Bond themed menu and killer cocktails! Great space for groups.

Date visited: _____

Went with: _____

Notes: _____

_____

_____

My rating: _____

Southpark Wine Bar

Downtown Map
901 SW Salmon
(503) 326-1300
www.southparkseafood.com

Happy Hours
3:00–6:00pm Daily

Food Deals 2
$3.00–$8.00
Happy Hour menu with a few regular menu items
at discounted prices, plus an array of small plates:
salad, soup, calamari, cheese plate, pizza, oysters.

Drink Specials 2
$4.00 red, white or sparkling wines
$4.00 glass of sangria ($10.00 carafe)

Atmosphere 3
Southpark has been a perennial favorite of many
a Portlander, myself included. It just works on so
many levels. Be aware that it's more of a bar than
a romantic wine-date place and that it can get
crowded. Outstanding wine selection.

Date visited: _____

Went with: _____

Notes: _____

_____

_____

My rating: _____

Teardrop Lounge

Pearl Map
1015 NW Everett
(503) 970-8331
www.teardroplounge.com

Happy Hours
4:00–7:00pm Daily

Food Deals 2
$4.00
Delicious line-up changes weekly
(choice of three gourmet selections – get all 3!)

Drink Specials 3
$1.00 off beer, wine and saké
$5.00 specialty weekly cocktail (choice of 2)

Atmosphere 3
Attention to detail in every aspect of design
almost brings a tear to my eye... It's gorgeous
every step of the way from the bartenders and
their magical mixology (the real focus), to the
industrial chic and very cool decor. LOVE it!

Date visited: ....

Went with: ....

Notes: ....

....

....

My rating: ....

Vintage Cocktail Lounge

Southeast (not on map)
7907 SE Stark
(503) 262-0696
www.vintagepdx.com

Happy Hours
5:00pm-7:00pm and 11:00pm–close Daily

Food Deals 2
$2.00–$5.00
Sustainable choices in food menu items: Choice
of six pizzettas, field greens salad, mixed olives.

Drink Specials 3
$3.00 drafts, $1.50 domestic tallboys, $4.00 wines
$2.50 wells; $5.00 barmaster cocktail of the day

Atmosphere 2
Part wine bar in style (formerly Cru Wine Bar)
and part old-school cocktail lounge with lots of
red in walls, lighting and everywhere. Casual
and welcoming.

Date visited: _____

Went with: _____

Notes: _____

_____

_____

My rating: _____

— Vault + Jinx —

For years, Vault Martini has been *the* place to go and enjoy cocktails! Sometimes it seems like the whole Pearl revolves around centrally-located Vault. And now it has a wonderful new neighbor! No food specials, but special attention is needed:

Vault Martini
Pearl Map
226 NW 12th Ave.; (503) 224-4909
www.vault-martini.com

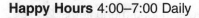

Happy Hours 4:00–7:00 Daily

Drink Specials 3
$4.00–$5.00 20+ cocktails (see full menu of 80+!)

Atmosphere 3 Surely, you must know it...
Fireplace, lounge areas, long bar, sidewalk action.

Jinx
Pearl Map
232 12th Ave.; (503) 224-0173
www.jinxlounge.com

Happy Hours 3:00–6:00 Daily

Drink Specials 3
$4.00–$5.00 20+ cocktails (with fun retro menus)

Atmosphere 3
Cool and laid-back retro vibe and decor without being over the top. Deep red walls adorned with funky artwork and fabulous flea market finds. Soft-glow lighting effects include very cool inverted lotus flowers and 1950s table lamps.

More Quick Sips

● ●

East www.eastchinatownlounge.com
Old Town Map 322 NW Everett; (503) 226-1569
5:00–9:00pm Tues–Fri: $1.00 off wells and beer
VERY cool red-light lounge—memorable & striking.
A personal favorite for mood and flattering light!

Invasion www.invasionpdx.com
Downtown Map 412 SW 4th Ave.; (503) 226-7777
4:00–7:00pm Daily: $3 wells; $4 wine; $5 cocktail
Totally mod, glam and retro club for boyfriends and
girlfriends. Snacks for $2 bucks at Happy Hour:
chex mix, roasted soybeans, cup o'balls, and salad.

Kir www.kirwinebar.com
Lloyd Center-ish Map 22 NE 7th; (503) 232-3063
No Happy Hour discounts. Simple, understated and
small, but apparently very romantic, wine bar.

Lupa www.lupawine.com
North/NE Map 3955 N Mississippi; (503) 287-5872
No Happy Hour discounts. Small and cozy, dark and
nice neighborhood wine bar with big wall of wine.

M Bar
NW/Nob Hill Map 417 NW 21st; (503) 228-6614
6:00–8:00pm Daily: $3.00 drafts and $3.00 wine
Romantic, tiny, candlelit lounge with outdoor patio.
A favorite secret treasure!

Paragon www.paragonrestaurant.com
Pearl Map 1309 NW Hoyt; (503) 833-5060
No discounts, but great place to grab a bite or drink.
A favorite Pearl hangout that's always crowded.

Secret Society Lounge

North/NE Map 116 NE Russell; (503) 493-3600
www.secretsociety.net
<u>5:00–7:00pm Daily</u> $1.00 off drinks; $5.00 cocktails
Chalkboard Happy Hour menu $3.00–$7.00
*Very cool space! I could tell you how great it is, but
then I'd have to kill you. Shhh... discover the mystery!*

Thatch Tiki Bar

Lloyd Map 2733 NE Broadway; (503) 281-8454
<u>5:00–6:30pm Tues–Sat; All day Sunday</u>
$5.00 mai-tais; $4.00 wells; $1.00 off beer
*Extreme personality with true respect and aesthetic
of 50's/60s style Tiki. No discounts on food.*

Veritable Quandary

Downtown (East) Map
1220 SW 1st Ave.; (503) 227-7342
www.vqpdx.com
*No discounts offered, but needs to be listed as it is
so often cited by the after-work crowd as a veritable
favorite. Bustling front outdoor patio beckons.*

Victory Bar

Southeast (Off Map)
3652 SE Division; (503) 236-8755
www.thevictorybar.com
<u>5:00–7:00pm Daily</u> $1 off drafts, $3 wells, $4 martinis
*Old-school interior and cocktails; one of the "100 Best
Places To Drink Beer In America" — Imbibe Magazine*

Vino Paradiso

Pearl Map 417 NW Tenth Ave.; (503) 295-9536
www.vinoparadiso.com
<u>4:00–6:00pm Tues–Sun</u> 1/2 off bottles of select wine
Another jewel in the Pearl with Utopian wine selection.

Also see the waterfront section! Great Happy Hours and
winebars: **Five Spice** on p. 234 and **Thirst** on p. 242.

Contemporary

Cool
Chic
&
Modern

Big-bucks city-style and the most impressive, "non-Portlandy" places in town. They are all kind of big and boxy, cool and contemporary. Best of all, they take their Happy Hours seriously, and offer delirious discounts on extra high-quality food and drinks. Many of my personal favorites are in this section! Except for Aloft's wxyz, they all get top marks, big cheers, and an attitude of gratitude for throwing down a kick-ass Happy Hour (Aloft needs to be here though, to remember it for that first drink when you pick up a friend from the airport, and its got the look). Other places with similar contemporary and stylish atmosphere, but for various reasons appear elsewhere in this book are Aquariva, Metrovino, Noble Rot, NV, and The Original.

23 Hoyt

NW/Nob Hill Map
529 NW 23rd Ave.
(503) 445-7400
www.23hoyt.com

Happy Hours
5:00–7:00pm Tues–Thurs;
5:00pm–6:30pm Fri–Sat

Food Deals 3
$1.00–$5.00
Several alternatives at each price point with
seasonal menu including a charcuterie plate,
cheeseburger, salads, soup, sliders, clams, fries.

Drink Specials 3
$2.00 draft beer; $5.00 red or white wine,
$5.00 specialty cocktails, martini, margarita

Atmosphere 3
Sleek, stylish and soaring inside with lofted
seating overlooking the bar area. Very cool design,
yet remains warm and inviting. Stellar!

Date visited: _____

Went with: _____

Notes: _____

_____

_____

My rating: _____

Aloft wxyz Bar

NE/Airport (Off Map)
9920 NE Cascade Parkway
(503) 200-5678
www.wxyzportland.com

Happy Hours
5:00–7:30pm Sun–Fri

Food Deals 1
$3.00
Three choices: salsa, guac & chips, tots, hummus

Drink Specials 1
$3.50 domestics; $4.25 microbrews
$6.00 house wines; $3.00 wells; $5.00 fizzy

Atmosphere 3+
Really cool space, but lame breaks for Happy
Hour and open to the bright lobby. Fascinating
glowing bar top puts on its own lightshow.
Geometric shapes everywhere and several
group sitting areas. The MAX line goes right there
(tricky directions via car)! Great place for groups
and parties. Check website for live music!

Date visited: _____

Went with: _____

Notes: _____

_____

_____

My rating: _____

Aura

1022 W Burnside
(503) 597-2872
www.auraportland.com

Happy Hours
5:00–7:00pm Wed–Sat

Food Deals 3
$2.00–$5.00
Big varied menu of 15 or so items including tiger
prawns, fish tacos, calamari, burgers, fries, wings,
salads, cheese fondue, poppers, empanadas.

Drink Specials 3
$3.00 featured drafts, wine and well drinks

Atmosphere 3
Enjoy the nightclub atmosphere with hi-tech
abstract light screens, white glowing bar, and
trapezoid tables in private curtained booths.
Don't miss the see-thru stylish bathrooms!

Date visited: _____

Went with: _____

Notes: _____

_____

_____

My rating: _____

Bay 13

Pearl Map
701 NW 13th Ave.
(503) 227-1133
www.bay13restaurant.com

Happy Hours
4:00–6:00pm Daily; 9:00pm–close Sun–Thurs
10:00pm–close Fri–Sat

Food Deals 2
$3.00–$8.00
Delicious menu with miso soup, edamame, fries,
mussels, calamari, foccacia and grilled flatbread.

Drink Specials 3
$5.00 draft beers, choice of several wines,
sparklings or pomegranate ginger martini

Atmosphere 3
An absolutely *huge* place with the look of the
Pearl-style industrial-mod down to a science.
The front-and-center bar is very slick and cool;
a bit of a see-and-be-seen place, but on the
more mellow scene at Happy Hour.

Date visited: _____

Went with: _____

Notes: _____

_____

_____

My rating: _____

Blue Hour

250 NW 13th Ave.
(503) 226-3394
www.bluehouronline.com

TOP TEN FAVORITE!

Happy Hours
4:30–6:30pm Daily (opens 5:00pm Sat)

Food Deals 3
$1.00–$5.00
Half-off extensive bar menu: bruschetta plate,
pizza, salad, fries, cheese plate, fondue, burgers,
spaghetti, Caesar salad, oyster shooters.

Drink Specials 3
$3.00 select draft beer; $20 select bottle wine
$6.00 specialty cocktails/martini

Atmosphere 3+
Impressive lofted interior; *very* well-designed—
a Portland standout! Trés trendy and active scene
(can be a touch loud). Happy Hour sidewalk patio
dining allowed—and totally enjoyed! Ultra cool
lighting effects at night. LOVE it!

Date visited: _____

Went with: _____

Notes: _____

_____

_____

My rating: _____

Candy

Happy Hours
3:00–7:00pm Mon-Sat;
9:00pm-close Wed–Thur ($7.00 meals w/drink)

Food Deals 3
$2.00–$5.00
Pizzas for only $3.00 bucks, and build-your-own burgers starting at $4.00! Plus deals on deli or grilled chicken sandwiches, sliders, wings, nachos.

Drink Specials 3
$3.00 house red and white wines; $3.00 wells
$4.00–6.00 range of specialty drinks
$5.00 Sunday (9am–4pm) Bloody Mary bar
.

Atmosphere 3+
They call it an "ultra-lounge" and it is most definitely all that! Very stylish, tantalizing and almost Vegas-y, see website for striking, shiny red visuals.

Date visited: _____

Went with: _____

Notes: _____

_____

_____

My rating: _____

Clark Lewis

• • • • • • • • • • • • • • • •

Central Eastside Map
1001 SE Water Ave.
(503) 235-2294
www.clarklewispdx.com

Happy Hours
5:00–6:30pm Mon–Sat

Food Deals 3
$1.00–$6.00
Seasonal menu of 15 or so choice nibbles:
soup, crostini, baby greens, artisan cheese
plate, croquettes, spaghetti, clams, burgers,
mac & cheese and dessert too!

Drink Specials 3
$3.00 draft; $4.50 house wine
$4.00 martini; $5.00 sidecar or gimlet

Atmosphere 3
Sophisticated renovation of old loading dock
with northwest and industrial-chic stylings; full,
long wall of streetscape gridded windows (open
or candlelit), big wooden tables for groups and
tucked-away two-tops. A perfect date place!

Date visited: _____

Went with: _____

Notes: _____

_____

_____

My rating: _____

Departure

Downtown Map
525 SW Morrison; Rooftop Bar
(503) 222-9996
www.departureportland.com

Happy Hours
4:00–6:00pm Tues–Sat

Food Deals 3
$3.00–$6.00
Mostly Asian-inspired menu with things like maki roll, edamame, miso soup, wings, plus BLT & mo'!

Drink Specials 3
$5.00 beer; $5.00 wine/bubbles ($20 bottle)
$5.00 cocktails/sake of the day

Atmosphere 3+
It's a departure from Portland norm in every way! From the funky elevator entrance and Space-Mountain-style exit, you know you're someplace different. Warm weather offers *three* top-floor patio seating areas with stellar views of the city below and mountains in the distance. Website has spectacular photography for a pre-tour.

Date visited: ....

Went with: ....

Notes: ....

....

....

My rating: ....

H5O Bistro

. . . .

8

Downtown (West) Map
50 SW Morrison
(503) 484-1415
www.h5obistro.com

Happy Hours
3:00–6:00pm and 9:00pm–close Mon–Sat;
★All day Sunday (11:00am–close)

Food Deals 2
$3.00–$8.00
A giant array of about 30 appetizers/meals! Great
prices all day, with only $1.00 off for Happy Hour:
burgers, salads, soups, empanadas, fritters, fries.

Drink Specials 2
$1.00 off beer, wine and wells

Atmosphere 3+
Ultra-mod with knock-out design: contrasts of
geometric shapes in decor and plates; sleek, clean,
and linear, yet inviting and friendly; open fireplace;
stellar ambiance! Great for groups.

Date visited: _____

Went with: _____

Notes: _____

_____

_____

My rating: _____

Ten|01

Pearl Map
1001 NW Couch
(503) 226-3463
www.ten-01.com

Happy Hours
3:00–6:00pm Mon–Sat

Food Deals 3
$1.00–$6.00 (half-off)
Fancy and delish food includes oysters, chorizo
or hamburger, truffle fries, nuts, and ice cream.

Drink Specials 3
$3.00 tap beer; $5.00 selected house cocktails
$5.00 red, white & sparkling wines

Atmosphere 3
High ceilings with a small-ish bar area. A fun
scene, and they built it green. Understated;
boxy, light and sleek.

Date visited: _____

Went with: _____

Notes: _____

_____

_____

My rating: _____

Urban Farmer

TOP TEN FAVORITE!

Downtown (East) Map
525 SW Morrison
(503) 222-4900
www.urbanfarmerrestaurant.com

Happy Hours
3:00–6:00pm and 10:00pm–close Daily

Food Deals 3
$2.00–$6.00
Totally revamped menu of farm-fresh NW delights with seasonal updates: tuna tartare, chicken, beef or pork sliders, fondue, fries, flatbread, chef's soup.

Drink Specials 3
$3.00 drafts; $5.00 house wines; $5.00 cocktail of the day and/or a fun "moonshine" punch

Atmosphere 3
Absolutely stunning! The number one decor award winner! Truly a Portland stand-out in the giant, cavernous atrium of the Hotel Nines with cozy, mini-atrium seating areas. Ultra-modern style with subtle rustic touches. Definitely coolest at night!

Date visited: _____

Went with: _____

Notes: _____

_____

_____

My rating: _____

Eclectic

Outside of the Box
and
Is it a Happy Hour?

The following pages review restaurants that defy specific categories. Not to quirky, not too extreme, and nice but not too fancy. Simply unique.

It also includes restaurants that defy Happy Hour convention, with Happy Hours that go all night.

Alleyway Café

2415 NE Alberta St.
(503) 287-7760

Happy Hours
3:00–7:00pm Daily

Food Deals 3 $2.00–$3.00 Fresh taste in long list of little nibbles with big discounts: 1/2 turkey sandwich, veggie platter, griled cheese, award-winning sweet potato fries, tacos, salad.

Drink Specials 3 $2.00 PBRs; $3.00 micros $4.00 mimosas, Bloody Marys or mojitos Only $2.00 for well drinks!

Atmosphere 2· Low-key and ultra-casual neighborhood café with artsy rotating gallery wares and outstanding outdoor space to imbibe.

Date visited: ....
Went with: ....
Notes: ....
....
....

My rating: ....

Basta's Trattoria

410 NW 21st Ave.
(503) 274-1572
www.bastastrattoria.com

Happy Hours
Food: 5:00pm–close Daily
Drinks: 5:00-6:30pm; 10:00pm-close Daily

Food Deals 2
$1.00–$7.00
Huge rotating menu with unusual samplings
along with basic standards: organic beet greens,
skewers, spaghetti, carpaccio, burgers, salads.

Drink Specials 2
$3.00 beers; $2.00 off glass of any wine
$5.00 well drinks

Atmosphere 2
Retro Italian on the down-low with high-up
mural paintings; kidney shapes and velvet
drapes; outdoor sidewalk seating.

Date visited: _____
Went with: _____
Notes: _____
_____
_____

My rating: _____

Café Nell

1987 NW Kearney
(503) 295-6487
www.cafenell.com

Happy Hours
3:00–6:00pm Tues–Fri; 4:00pm–close Sat ★

Food Deals 3
$1.00–$5.00
Big and diverse menu includes their famous
omelet & fries, chili lime shrimp, three kinds of
sliders, BBQ riblets, skewers, salad, grits, soup
(FYI, they also serve a great breakfast and lunch).

Drink Specials 2
$2.00 beer or Lillet; $4.00 martinis; $4.00 bubbles

Atmosphere 3
Cute, little hidden gem tucked away on a quiet
tree-lined street. A welcoming brasserie both day
and night. Tiny Parisian-style bar with big cushy
couch and cafe windows opening to the outside.

Date visited: _____

Went with: _____

Notes: _____

_____

_____

My rating: _____

Caldera Public House

Southeast (off Map)
6031 SE Stark
(503) 233-8242
www.calderapublichouse.com

Happy Hours
5:00–6:00pm & 9:00pm–close Daily

Food Deals 2
$3.00–$9.00
Short list of bar menu items like fries, tots, garlic bread, hummus plate, calamari, coconut shrimp.

Drink Specials 2
$1.00 off pints, wine, wells and cocktails

Atmosphere 3
Kinda hidden over in the far east, but this little Montavilla neighborhood is starting to sprout some new favorites. Inside a turn-of-the-century, two-story drugstore, Caldera reminds me both of my old Chicago taverns and some in Ireland. It has character! And a great back deck too.

Date visited: _____
Went with: _____
Notes: _____
_____
_____

My rating: _____

Casa Naranja

4205 N Mississippi
(503) 459-4049
www.casanaranjapdx.com

Happy Hours
4:00–6:00pm Daily; 10:00pm–close Mon–Sat

Food Deals 2
$2.00–$6.00
Seasonal menu rotates (it's not Mexican food as the name may lead you to think): bacon wrapped scallops, burritos, squash soup, salad.

Drink Specials 3
$1.50 PBR tall boys; $1.00 off drafts
$1.00 off house wines; $3.00 wells

Atmosphere 3
Super cute, very *orange* two story Victorian house. Homey touches inside with original artwork, candles and fresh flowers; but it's all about the front, back and side deck and patio areas complete with tiki torches and umbrellas.

Date visited: _____

Went with: _____

Notes: _____

_____

_____

My rating: _____

Clyde Common

Downtown (West) Map
1014 SW Stark
(503) 228-3333
www.clydecommon.com

Happy Hours
3:00–6:00pm Mon–Fri
11:00pm–close Mon–Sat (food only)

Food Deals 3
$3.00–$6.00
Bigger menu includes both unique and main-
stream treats like popcorn, salad, grilled onion
goat cheese panini, burger, flatbread, cookies.

Drink Specials 2
$3.50 drafts; $5.00 fun and funky cocktails

Atmosphere 3
Big, open warehouse space like an unfinished
art school gallery. Rough wood floors, banged
up bar stools, stenciled signage, and butcher
paper walls give it a working-man edge.

Date visited: _____

Went with: _____

Notes: _____

_____

_____

My rating: _____

Crown Room

9

Old Town Map
205 NW 4th Ave.
(503) 222-6655
www.thecrownroom.net

Happy Hours
5:00-7:00pm Tues–Fri

Food Deals 2
$3.00–$5.00
Choose from a dozen appetizers including spanakopita, stuffed mushrooms, artichoke romano, lemon chicken, buffalo wings, chicken quesadilla, shrimp cocktail, sirloin beef tips.

Drink Specials 3
$3.00 drafts; wine, wells; $6.00 specialty cocktails

Atmosphere 3
This place really *is* "old school lounging at its best!" Large, open nightclub space with lots of 50s-style vinyl, oversized lounge booths, dim lighting, and a stage for Elvis impersonators.

Date visited: _____

Went with: _____

Notes: _____

_____

_____

My rating: _____

Crush

Southeast Map
1412 SE Morrison
(503) 235-8150
www.crushbar.com

Happy Hours
4:30–7:00pm Tues–Sun
★All day Tuesdays (food only later 'til 11:00pm)

Food Deals 3
$2.50–$5.50
Expanded menu of Happy Hour food with many items added, like yams w/curry sauce (vegans *love it*), baba ganoush, quesadillas, flat nachos.

Drink Specials 3
$3.00 microbrews; $4.50 house wines
$3.00–$3.50 wells; $4.50 cocktails

Atmosphere 2
Open, artsy lounge with stunning bottle chandelier; a favorite neighborhood hangout.

Date visited: _____

Went with: _____

Notes: _____

_____

_____

My rating: _____

Equinox

● ●

North/NE Map
830 N Shaver St
(503) 460-3333
www.equinoxrestaurantpdx.com

Happy Hours
4:00–6:00pm Tues–Fri

Food Deals 3
$2.00–$6.50
Short but sweet menu: wild mushroom wontons
(yum!), fettucini, pork taco, cheddar-burger, fries,
calamari, Caesar salad, mussels.

Drink Specials 3
$3.00 drafts; $4.00 wine; $3.50 wells
$4.50 specialty cocktails

Atmosphere 3
Enter through their delightful front patio (where
you can enjoy Happy Hour weather permitting).
Inside, it's warm and woody throughout with old,
rough wood floors, natural wood tables, and
paneled half-walls. Skylight and garage door.

Date visited: _____

Went with: _____

Notes: _____

_____

_____

My rating: _____

Gotham Tavern

2240 N Interstate
(503) 517-9911
www.gothamtavern.com

Happy Hours
4:00–7:00pm and 9:00pm–close Daily

Food Deals 2
$3.00
Small, but tasty menu of spicy buffalo wings, pepperjack quesadilla, lettuce wraps, artichoke dip with sun-dried tomatoes and shrimp ceviche

Drink Specials 2
$3.00 select draft; $2.00 PBRs $4.00 wells
Occasional other nightly specials

Atmosphere 3
Amazing, artistic woodwork divides bar from dining room and if you're lucky, you'll get a rare opportunity to drink and dine inside your own private egg (see for yourself). Outside HH too. Prime location for Rose Quarter pre-show fun!

Date visited: _____

Went with: _____

Notes: _____

_____

_____

My rating: _____

Hobo's

120 NW 3rd Ave.
(503) 224-3285
www.hobospdx.com

Happy Hours
4:00–6:30pm Mon–Fri

Food Deals 2
$3.00–$4.00
Classic pub grub done well: calamari, fish tacos, buffalo hot wings, oyster shooters, cheese fries, quesadilla, and mac & cheese.

Drink Specials 2
$1.00 off beer and wells; $5.00 wine
$5.00 specialty cocktails

Atmosphere 3
Beautiful, turn-of-the-century, old Portland charm; positioned directly over the haunted Shanghai Tunnels and the starting point for the ghostly Portland Underground Tours (www.shanghai tunnels.info). Built in 1885.

Date visited: _____

Went with: _____

Notes: _____

_____

_____

My rating: _____

Holden's Bistro

Pearl Map
524 NW 14th Ave.
(503) 916-0099
www.holdensbistro.com

Happy Hours
5:00–7:00pm Mon–Sat

Food Deals 3
$3.00–$6.00
Happy Hour basics done up extra-deliciously:
burgers, three kinds of french fries, pulled pork
tacos, hummus plate, spinach artichoke dip.

Drink Specials 2
$1.00 off beer and wine
$5.00–$6.50 house cocktails

Atmosphere 3
Sleek, boxy and masculine loft-style lounge.
Warm in winter's dark nights with a wall of flick-
ering candles and glowing bottles behind the
bar. Cool in the summer with outside seats and
open air "garage" door.

Date visited: _____

Went with: _____

Notes: _____

_____

_____

My rating: _____

Imbibe

Southeast
2229 SE Hawthorne
(503) 239-4002

Happy Hours
4:00-7:00pm Mon-Sat; 10:00-close Mon-Thur, Sat
★All day Sunday (4:00pm–close)

Food Deals 3
$3.00–$5.00
Huge bar menu with many Thai specialties too:
angus slider sampler, salad rolls, mac & cheese,
skewers, potstickers, fries, salad, soup.

Drink Specials 2
75 cents off beer (thus $1.50–$3.50)
$3.00 well drinks

Atmosphere 3
Metropolitan, swanky, chic decor; wall-size
windows open to outside; good (but very loud)
live music occasionally at Happy Hour.

Date visited: _____
Went with: _____
Notes: _____

_____

My rating: _____

Jimmy Mak's

Pearl Map
221 NW 10th Ave
(503) 295-6542
www.jimmymaks.com

Happy Hours
5:00–7:00pm Mon–Sat

Food Deals 3
$5.00
Revamped and improved menu with good-sized portions and variety of items like bacon-wrapped prawns, spanokopita, gyros, pizzas, and salads.

Drink Specials 1
$1.00 off pints and wells

Atmosphere 3
Be an early bird and enjoy Jimmy Mak's swanky jazz club finery complete with thick, brilliantly illuminated red velvet curtains, dark & cushy booth seating, and tiny candle-lit cocktail tables. And while you're there, play some free pool too!

Date visited: _____

Went with: _____

Notes: _____

_____

_____

My rating: _____

Living Room Theaters

• • • • • • • • • • • • • • • • • • • •

Downtown (West) Map
341 SW 10th Ave.
(971) 222-2005
www.livingroomtheaters.com

Happy Hours
4:00–6:00pm Mon–Fri; 10:00pm–close Sun–Thur

Food Deals 2
$4.00
Delicious, inexpensive and healthy movie food:
Small menu of Spanish-style tortillas, mezza plate,
pizza, chicken skewers, or turkey sandwiches.

Drink Specials 3
$3.00 beer; $4.00 white and red wine
$6.00 martini

Atmosphere 3
Sleek, urban/retro stylings with low tables,
fuzzy pillows and glowing, backlit "mood" bar;
enjoy top-quality high-def movies in recliners
with drink in hand. Get on their email list!

Date visited: ....

Went with: ....

Notes: ....

....

....

My rating: ....

Maiden

Southeast
639 SE Morrison
(503) 232-5553
www.themaidenpdx.com

Happy Hours
4:00–6:30pm Mon–Sat; All night Tuesday★

Food Deals 3
$3.00–$8.00
Big menu with fresh, unique items, generous
portion sizes and slight Spanish spin: ceviche,
fish tacos, fish & chips, duck quesadilla, salads,
Painted Hills burger, soup, Spanish meatballs.

Drink Specials 3
$3.00 choice tap; $5.00 House wine or sangria;
$1.00 PBR tall boys, $3.50 wells

Atmosphere 2
Nostalgic, sea-wench style with faded ship
paintings and gilded frames, Oriental rugs,
unique bar lighting and sidewalk patio tables.

Date visited: _____

Went with: _____

Notes: _____

_____

_____

My rating: _____

Melting Pot

•••••••••••••••••••••

9

Downtown (East) Map
1001 5th Ave. (entrance at 6th & Main)
(503) 517-8960
www.meltingpot.com

Happy Hours
4:00-6:30pm Mon–Fri

Food Deals 3
$2.00–$5.00 (plus $12.00 cheese fondues)
Big discounts on great food: several salad
selections ($3.00 each); artichoke and spinach
dip; shrimp cocktail; smoked salmon cheese ball;
mushroom paté; lobster, shrimp and caviar cups.

Drink Specials 3
$3.00 draft beer; $5.50 red wine
$5.00 white wine; $5.50 daily cocktail

Atmosphere 2
Subterranean entrance leads to clean and simple
windowless batcave perfect for celebrating
cold winter nights or escaping summer heat.
More stark and sleek than romantic, but dark.

Date visited: _____

Went with: _____

Notes: _____

_____

_____

My rating: _____

Mississippi Station

8

3943 N Mississippi
(503) 517-5751
www.mississippistation.com

Happy Hours
3:00pm–6:00pm and 9:00–10:00pm Tues–Sun

Food Deals 3
$3.00–$7.00
Big small-plate menu includes chicken wings,
soup and bread, polish dog, garlic fries, sliders,
salads, tapas plate, and pizza.

Drink Specials 2
$3.00 microbrews pints; $1.00 off wells & wine

Atmosphere 2
Big, meandering patio illuminated with twinkling
Italian lights. Surrounded by wooden fencing,
it's an absolutely perfect beer garden. Inside
is warm and casual with old station charm.

Date visited: _____

Went with: _____

Notes: _____

_____

_____

My rating: _____

North 45

NW/Nob Hill Map
517 NW 21st Ave.
(503) 248-6317
www.north45pub.com

Happy Hours
4:00–6:00pm Daily; All night on Mondays★
Plus 11:00pm–2:00am Wed

Food Deals 3
$2.50–$6.00
Small menu, but tasty appetizers like calamari,
wings, mac & cheese, steak & shrooms, salads,
and pomme frites (yum!)

Drink Specials 2
$3.50 pints of draft pilsner; $5.00-$8.00 wines
$4.00 wells; $5.00 "Patio-Rita"

Atmosphere 3
A rich, but homey feel to their travelers-themed
bar with framed maps and vacation photos.
Very cozy inside/huge patio beer garden in back
– which is tented and heated in the winter!

Date visited: _____

Went with: _____

Notes: _____

_____

_____

My rating: _____

Perry's

2401 NE Fremont
(503) 287-3655
www.perrysonfremont.com

Happy Hours
4:00–6:00pm Tues–Sat

Food Deals 3
$2.95 all items
Field green salad, flatbread w/goat cheese,
chicken tacos, sesame Thai chicken, vegetable
enchilada, nachos, Caesar, mini burger, mac
& cheese, spaghetti, tostadas.

Drink Specials 1
Occasional nightly drink special

Atmosphere 3
Like a traveler/artist's home; impressive iron
work greeting, masks, decorated atrium sky
lights, paintings, ethnic and art statues. Cute
patio in nice weather!

Date visited: _____

Went with: _____

Notes: _____

_____

_____

My rating: _____

The Press Club

10

Southeast Map
2621 SE Clinton
(503) 233-5656
www.myspace.com/thepressclub

Happy Hours
3:00–6:00pm Mon–Fri; ★Mondays 'til 11:00pm
Tuesdays 1/2 price wine selection 6:00–11:00pm

Food Deals 3
$3.00–$5.00
Fresh salads and soup; crepes or sandwiches
(named after famous authors).

Drink Specials 3
$1.00 off beer and wine (i.e. $2.50 imports!)
$5.00 cocktails; plus nightly specials and coffee

Atmosphere 3
If the ever-so-treasured Powell's Bookstore was
a small neighborhood bar, it would be The
Press Club. There's a sweet, laid-back vibe here
that works well if you are a fan of coffee houses,
bookstores, Paris, or hipster concert venues.

Date visited: ....

Went with: ....

Notes: ....

....

....

My rating: ....

Silk

Pearl Map
1012 NW Glisan
(503) 248-2172
www.silkbyphovan.com

Happy Hours
4:00–9:30pm Mon–Sat ★

Food Deals 2
$5.00–$7.00
Very tasty but pricey Vietnamese mini-dinners
including salad rolls, crispy rolls, hoisin ribs,
chicken curry, lemongrass chicken, toastettes,
wings, crazy noodles and soups.

Drink Specials 2
$4.00 Kirin beer, $6.00 specialty cocktails
$6.00 red or white wine

Atmosphere 3
White and natural borderline-retro decor blends
contemporary hard lines with silky flow. It's
totally mod, gorgeous, and romantic.

Date visited: _____
Went with: _____
Notes: _____
_____
_____

My rating: _____

Three Doors Down

SE/Hawthorne Map
1429 SE 37th Ave
(503) 236-6886
www.3doorsdowncafe.com

Happy Hours
★All night (5:00–10:00pm) Tues–Thur and Sun

Food Deals 3
$2.00–$10.00
Big chalkboard menu of delicious, somewhat
Italian-focused specials like fettucine, tortiglione,
zuppa de mare, stuffed peppers, mac & cheese.

Drink Specials 2
$4.50 house wines; $5.00 manhattans / martinis
(Beware $5.50 beers *not* included in Happy Hour)

Atmosphere 3
Woo hoo! Three Doors Down broke down and is
offering Happy Hour in the bar area. Not quite as
cute and quiet as the door-decorated restaurant
side, but has a similar, romantically social, wine
bar vibe. Enjoy it all night!

Date visited: _____

Went with: _____

Notes: _____

_____

_____

My rating: _____

Voicebox Karaoke

NW/Nob Hill Map
2112 NW Hoyt
(503) 303-8220
www.voiceboxpdx.com

Happy Hours
4:00–7:00pm Tues–Sun ($4.00/hr. Karaoke)
Tuesdays 7:00pm–11:00pm $10.00 covers karaoke

Food Deals 2
$3.00–$6.50
Small but tasty and unique menu of dumplings
(vegan, pork or bacon cheeseburger), steamed
edamame, plus shredded squid jerky and candy!

Drink Specials 2
$1.00 off beer and select saké
$5.00 select house wine

Atmosphere 3
New concept in karaoke bars—rent private "boxes"
and never stop singing (or laughing as the case
may be—it's a blast!). High-style space-age
Japanese pop decor with Pander Bros. art, ultra-
mod hanging lamps and high-def big-screen TVs.

Date visited: _____

Went with: _____

Notes: _____

_____

_____

My rating: _____

Wild Abandon

Southeast Map
2411 SE Belmont
(503) 232-4458
www.wildabandonrestaurant.com

Happy Hours
4:30–6:30pm Mon, Wed–Fri

Food Deals 3
$1.00-$4.95
Choose from over 17 gourmet specialties including soup, au gratin or mashed potatoes, shrimp or chicken with polenta, pastas, flank steak, burger. (Plus nightly specials from a real dinner menu!)

Drink Specials 3
$2.00–$3.00 beer; $4.25 wine, sangrai or well drinks; $5.00–$6.00 cocktail specialties

Atmosphere 3
A funky little "Love Shack" as viewed from the street, things change inside to the romantic "Red Velvet Lounge," with both cozy dining indoors and a wonderful garden patio in back.

Date visited: _____

Went with: _____

Notes: _____

_____

_____

My rating: _____

Windows

●●●●●●●●●●●●●●●●●●●●●●●

8

1021 NE Grand (Top Floor Red Lion)
(503) 235-2100

Happy Hours
4:00–7:00pm Mon–Sun

Food Deals 2
$2.00–$5.00
Good but small menu of bar food: sushi rolls,
Caesar salad, spinach dip, soup, shrimp tempura,
beef satay, wings.

Drink Specials 2
$2.00–$5.00 nightly specials

Atmosphere 3
Skyline and river views, sunsets, and outdoor
deck – all very near Convention Center and
Rose Garden Arena in the Red Lion Hotel. Who
knew?! Kinda hotel-y inside, but nice out on the
patio in the summer!

Date visited: _____

Went with: _____

Notes: _____

_____

_____

My rating: _____

Club 915 www.club915pdx.com

Downtown Map 915 SW 2nd Ave.; (503) 274-0915

Happy Hours 3:00–7:00pm Daily

Food Deals 2 $1.50–$5.00 Insanely-huge bar menu of pretty much everything from fries to taquitos.

Drink Specials 1 $5.00 house wines

Atmosphere 3 Beautiful and huge brick space that has housed several recent restaurants, but is now a touch more bar-ish. Upstairs club has a keeping-it-real, in-the-house look (think HGTV).

Savoy Tavern www.savoypdx.com

SE Map 2500 SE Clinton; (503) 808-9999

Happy Hours 5:00–7:00pm & 10:00pm–close Daily

Food Deals 2 $2.00 Nostalgic Americana menu with their famous fried cheese curds, brats, burgers, fries, meatballs, smoked trout, deviled eggs, mac & cheese.

Drink Specials 3 $3.00 beer; $4.00 wine; $3.00 wells; $5.00 cocktails – plus nightly specials

Atmosphere 2 The bar has character! Kitchy 1950s lodge look by day, but cute & romantic candlelit at night.

Virgo & Pisces www.virgoandpisces.com

NW/Nob Hill Map 500 NW 21st; (503) 517-8855

Happy Hours ★3:00–close Sun–Thurs★; (3-7 drinks) 3:00–7:00pm and 9:30pm–close Fri–Sat

Food Deals 2 $3.00–$5.00
Nice array of delicious bar eats: scallop cigars, fish & chips, burgers; Many gluten-free alternatives.

Drink Specials 3 $3.00 drafts; $4.00 house wines; $4.00 martinis & saketinis

Atmosphere 2 Small, contemporary, stark & dark bar with huge hi-def TV. Very neat with a mutable mood.

International

Asian

Español

French

German

Indian

Irish

Italian

Mediterranean

Enjoy an array of various ethnic dishes from the four corners of the world! Feeling spicy? Feeling French? Want pasta? Take a culinary trip — without traveling!

Anju

3808 N Williams "C"
(503) 282-1063
www.anjupdx.com

Happy Hours
5:00–7:00pm Tues–Sat

Food Deals 3
$3.00
Unique and flavorful! Japanese/Korean small
plates like kimchi with bacon, or in pancakes
or dumplings; spicy wings or crab cakes; salad.

Drink Specials 2
$2.00 PBR, $4.00 Sapporo draft; $4.00 wines
$5.00 bartender's cocktail of the day

Atmosphere 3
Nice, serene little spot in one of those industrial
warehouse-style spaces in the HUB building.
Concrete mixes with dark brown walls, candlelight,
funky lava-like lamps, string art, and rusty
corrugated tin. Roller garage opens to street.

Date visited: _____

Went with: _____

Notes: _____

_____

_____

My rating: _____

Bamboo Sushi

●●●●●●●●●●●●●●●●●●●●●●●●●●●●

Lloyd Center-ish Map
310 SE 28th Ave.
(503) 232-5255
www.bamboosushipdx.com

Happy Hours
5:00–6:30pm Mon–Fri

Food Deals 3
$1.00–$5.00
Formerly known as Masu East, Bamboo Sushi
also has the best sushi in town: nigiri set, inari,
California rolls, daily hand rolls, vegetable roll.

Drink Specials 1
Rotating nightly special like a $6.00 cocktail

Atmosphere 3
Small, serene and cozy with focus on sustain-
ability and Japanese simplicity. Dark browns,
tans and white; carpeted with patterned pillows
on bench seating and fascinating origami fish art.

Date visited: _____

Went with: _____

Notes: _____

_____

_____

My rating: _____

Bambuza

● ●

8

3682 SW Bond Ave.
(503) 206-6330
Also locations in Tualatin and Seattle
www.bambuza.com

Happy Hours
3:00–6:00pm Mon–Sat

Food Deals 3
$2.00–$4.00
About a dozen delicious Vietnamese small
plates like salad and spring rolls, skewers,
soups, wontons, coconut shrimp and salads.

Drink Specials 3
$3.00 NW bottled beers; $4.00 house wines
$5.00 Martinis, Bellini fizz or mojito

Atmosphere 2
Colorful and bright, simple, quiet Asian bistro.
Open room with hanging orange lanterns,
green walls with bamboo stalks, lots of light
from two walls of windows.

Date visited: ....

Went with: ....

Notes: ....

....

....

My rating: ....

ASIAN

Bo Restobar

Downtown (East) Map
400 SW Broadway
(503) 222-2688
www.borestobar.com

Happy Hours
4:00–6:00pm and 9:00pm–mid Mon–Fri

Food Deals 3
$1.95–$6.95
Big menu full of super-yummy Asian delights!
Edamame, wings, sweet potato tempura, lemon-grass chowder, ribs, tofu, BoBurger sliders.

Drink Specials 3
$2.95 Draft Beer; $3.95 House Wine
$4.95 Cocktail of the Day

Atmosphere 3
Cozy nightclub vibe next to the Hotel Lucia.
Excellent design, lighting and color make it a
stand-out in Portland restaurant decor.

Date visited: ....

Went with: ....

Notes: ....

....

....

My rating: ....

Dragonfish

909 SW Park
(503) 243-5991
www.dragonfishcafe.com

Happy Hours
4:00–6:00pm and 10:00pm–close Mon–Sat
★All Day Sunday (3:00pm–close)

Food Deals 3
$1.95 nigiri (7 single-piece choices)
$1.95–$4.00 sushi rolls (5 four-piece plates)
$3.50–$4.00 small plates including potstickers,
lettuce cups, miso soup, carmel-ginger chicken

Drink Specials 3
$2.00 beers; $4.00 house wines; $2.00 saké
$4.00 Rubyrita or Lime Rickey

Atmosphere 3
The fun bar side of the restaurant (across the
hall) has bamboo, art, a wall of Pachinko game
machines, comfy couch seating, and hanging
metal art sculptures of sea creatures, with red
blinds and shoji screens.

Date visited: ....

Went with: ....

Notes: ....

....

....

My rating: ....

E-San Thai

●●●●●●●●●●●●●●●●●●●●●●●●●●●●

Downtown (East) Map
133 SW 2nd Ave
(503) 223-4090
www.e-santhai.com

Happy Hours
4:00–6:00pm and 9:00pm–close Daily

Food Deals 3
$2.50–$4.00
A whopping 18 Thai basics: egg rolls, wontons,
shrimp, squid, steamed clams/mussels, an array
of satays, fish cakes, coconut prawns, fried rice,
pad se ew and pad thai, pad kee mao and more.

Drink Specials 3
$2.00 Drafts(!); $3.50 well drinks

Atmosphere 2
Casual, comfortable, colorful Thai restaurant
without any over-the-top styling, but up-top dining
space for the huge crowds flooding in at lunch
hour (a sign of good food? I think so).

Date visited: ....

Went with: ....

Notes: ....

....

....

My rating: ....

Le Hana

• •

8

Waterfront Map
3500 SW River Parkway
(503)467-7533
www.lehana.com

Happy Hours
★4:30–6:00pm Mon–Fri; ★8:30pm–close Daily

Food Deals 3
$1.00–$5.00
Huge menu currently offers 23 tasty nibbles:
10 sushi items (rolls and nigiri); fried tofu, wings
or calamari; miso soup, several salads, mixed
tempura, veggie gyoza, sweet potato fries.

Drink Specials 1
$1.00 off beer and wells

Atmosphere 3
Elegant, inviting space blending diverse design
elements: simply beautiful floral arrangements,
large blocky sandstone bricks, tiny hanging red
globe lamps, silky white bar back, frosted floral
etched glass and a Rothko-esque wall mural.

Date visited: _____

Went with: _____

Notes: _____

_____

_____

My rating: _____

Masu

Downtown (West) Map
406 SW 13th Ave;
(503) 221-6278
www.masusushi.com

Happy Hours
3:00–6:00pm Daily; 10:00–11:00pm Mon–Thurs
11:00pm–midnight Fri–Sat

Food Deals 3+
$3.00–$7.00
Possibly the best sushi in the city! Big menu
of 12 items includes daily nigiri and rolls, tofu,
tempura, salads and wings.

Drink Specials 1
$3.00 Sapporo

Atmosphere 3
Unique "retro-Asian" lounge; open and boxy with
Jenga-style wood blocks covering the walls and
back bar; stunning, colorful, hand-painted mural.
Ultra cool!

Date visited: ....

Went with: ....

Notes: ....

....

....

My rating: ....

PF Chang's

Pearl Map
1139 NW Couch; (503) 432-4000
Tigard
7463 SW Bridgeport Road; (503) 430-3020
Hillsboro (Tanasbourne)
19320 NW Emma Way; (503) 533-4580
www.pfchangs.com

Happy Hours
3:00-6:00pm Daily

Food Deals 3
$3.00–$4.00
Half-off extensive list of appetizers! Delicious
selection of items like chicken lettuce wraps,
crab wontons, ahi tuna, calamari, and BBQ ribs.

Drink Specials 3
$3.00 drafts; $5.00-$6.00 wine; $5.00 cocktails

Atmosphere 3
An Emperor's Palace appearance, complete
with huge stone lion sculptures and artistic
modern lighting effects. Sit and enjoy the beauty
of the restaurant (kids are welcome) or the bar.

Date visited: _____

Went with: _____

Notes: _____

_____

_____

My rating: _____

Ping

Pearl Map
102 NW 4th Ave
(503) 229-7464
www.pingpdx.com

Happy Hours
2:00–5:30pm Mon-Fri

Food Deals 2
$2.00-$5.00
Changes seasonally based on menu favorites,
with items like steamed pork buns, skewers
(chicken, prawns, octopus or potato), ramen.

Drink Specials 3
$3.00 drafts (20 oz.); $4.00 select saké
$5.00 house specialty cocktails

Atmosphere 2
Long and low, front-and-center bar in front of
the open kitchen gives Ping an old American
diner look. Antique Chinese metal beverage
signs and hanging paper scupltures start to add
an Asian twist. Too bright at Happy Hour time.

Date visited: _____

Went with: _____

Notes: _____

_____

_____

My rating: _____

Saucebox

• • • • • • • • • • • • • • • • • • •

Downtown (East) Map
214 SW Broadway
(503) 241-3393
www.saucebox.com

Happy Hours
4:30–6:30pm Sun–Fri; 5:00–6:30 Sat

Food Deals 3
$1.00–$5.00
Huge menu of mostly Asian-inspired fusion dishes:
peanut noodles, satay, pad thai, salad and spring
rolls, fries, edamame, tataki (rare ahi), beet salad,
miso soup, and the best burgers!

Drink Specials 3
$3.00 select beer; $5.00 daily cocktail
$4.00 wine and saké; $4.00 boxcar or daiquiri

Atmosphere 3
Big & open, boxy, saucy lounge; chocolate browns
and greys; looming giant art murals lend more
personality to entire room. Cool bathroom entrance.

Date visited: ....

Went with: ....

Notes: ....

....

....

My rating: ....

Seres

● ● ● ● ● ● ● ● ● ● ● ● ● ● ● ● ● ● ●

Pearl Map
1105 NW Lovejoy
(971) 222-7327
www.seresrestaurant.com

Happy Hours
3:00–7:00pm Mon–Sat; 9:00–11:00pm Fri–Sat

Food Deals 3
$2.50–$5.00
Cravable Pan Asian delights like pot stickers, calamari, General Tso's chicken, spring or salad rolls, wontons, scallops, lo mein, fried rice.

Drink Specials 2
$3.00 drafts; $5.00 wines
$6.00 signature cocktails (22 choices!)

Atmosphere 3
Pearlesque loft-style with Far East reserve; small bar area with super-high ceiling and full window; natural tones and tables; gorgeous hanging tile art pieces. Formerly Sungari Pearl.

Date visited: _____

Went with: _____

Notes: _____

_____

_____

My rating: _____

Siam Society

TOP TEN FAVORITE!

2703 NE Alberta
(503) 922-3675
www.siamsociety.com

Happy Hours
4:30–6:30pm Mon–Fri; All night Tuesday★
Happy Hour food all the time in back lounge

Food Deals 3
$1.95–$6.95
Extreme delicious-ness in Thai Happy Hour food!
Pad Thai, grilled steak, pizza, coconut prawns,
salad rolls, grilled sausage. Lounge menu too.

Drink Specials 3
$2.75 drafts; $4.00 house wines; $3.50 wells

Atmosphere 3
Big city award-winning design in lofty old power
station; one of the coolest looks in Portland and
one of the best outdoor patios too. Check out
their more casual "bar" alternative out back —
the Soi Cowboy Lounge.

Date visited: ....

Went with: ....

Notes: ....

....

....

My rating: ....

Sweet Basil (Basil Bar)

7

●●●●●●●●●●●●●●●●●●●●●●●●●

Lloyd Center-ish
3135 NE Broadway; (503) 281-8337
NW/Nob Hill Map
1639 NW Glisan St.; (503) 473-8758
www.sweetbasilor.com

Happy Hours
4:30–6:30pm Mon–Fri; 4:30–9:00pm Sun★

Food Deals 3
$2.50–$4.75
WOW! YUM! Lots of delicious Thai specials:
OMG crab rolls, wraps, tofu/veggie or beef
salads, wings, crab rangoon, and wontons.

Drink Specials 1
Spendy but very unique cocktails on Broadway
Glisan beer and wine only (no discount)

Atmosphere 2
<u>Broadway:</u> Out of a Thai IKEA showroom; large
screen TV with couches; mysterious lounge-y
back room. <u>Glisan:</u> More colorful, albeit a bit
basic, but fun with windows in the bar area.

Date visited: _____

Went with: _____

Notes: _____

_____

_____

My rating: _____

Typhoon

410 SW Broadway; (503) 224-8285
www.typhoonrestaurants.com

Happy Hours
3:00-6:00pm Mon–Fri

Food Deals 3
$3.00 or $5.00
Big menu different than nextdoor's BoRestobar:
Papaya salad, edamame, onion rings, spring
rolls, poppers, prawns, pad thai, wonton or tom
kah soups, calamari with sweet & sour sauce.

Drink Specials 3
$3.00 select bottled beer; $4.00 house wines
$5.00 cocktail of the day

Atmosphere 3
Contemporary and serene decor; giant, marble
Buddha head illuminated at entry; glowing
orange glass bar top; striking wall of masks;
all surrounded by candlelight.

Date visited: _____
Went with: _____
Notes: _____
_____
_____

My rating: _____

Yakuza

Northeast (Off map)
5411 NE 30th Ave
(503) 450-0893
www.yakuzalounge.com

Happy Hours
5:30–7:00pm Mon–Sat; 5:30pm–Sunday★

Food Deals 3
$3.00–$5.00
A touch pricey for HH, but the quality is there!
Select several sushis from the cute litltle menu
that changes periodically and always fresh.
Nigri, salad, and large-size, hand-rolled sushi.

Drink Specials 1
$1.00 off beer and wells

Atmosphere 3
This Japanese pub is yet another masterpiece
created by Micah Camden of Beast, DOC and
Fats Pub fame, all in the same neighborhood.
Interior has simple wooden bench seating with
hanging draperies to softly separate spaces.
Beautiful, colorful murals adorn walls. Nice patio!

Date visited: _____

Went with: _____

Notes: _____

_____

_____

My rating: _____

Andina

Pearl Map
1314 NW Glisan
(503) 228-9535
www.andinarestaurant.com

Happy Hours
4:00–6:00pm Daily

Food Deals 2
$2.00 each
Skewer pairs for $2 bucks—can't go wrong with that! Choose from marinated chicken, beef heart, or grilled octopus. $1.50 raw bar oysters.

Drink Specials 2
$6.00 house wines; $6.75 Delicious variety of south-of-the border concoctions

Atmosphere 3
More center-city Lima than old-world Machu Picchu in tone; high wooden beamed ceilings, copper-topped tables, painted stucco walls, captivating fireplace. One of Portland's most renowned restaurants.

Date visited: _____

Went with: _____

Notes: _____

_____

_____

My rating: _____

Casa Del Matador

NW/Nob Hill Map
1438 NW 23rd Ave.; (503) 228-2855
2424 East Burnside; (503) 719-5757
www.matadorrestaurants.com

Happy Hours
4:00–6:00pm & 10:00pm–1:00am Daily

Food Deals 3
$4.00–$5.00
Big menu with better basics including quesadillas, nachos, calamari, chili, salad, tacos, soup, prawns, Tex-Mex spring rolls, hot wings.

Drink Specials 0
No drink specials, but know that they have over 75 varieties of tequila!

Atmosphere 3
A handsome and sexy interior worthy of the title "Matador" greets you at entrance with stunning, wrought iron artistry, gilded mirrors and rustic stucco walls. Compelling, centrally located circular fireplace perfect for groups.

Date visited: _____

Went with: _____

Notes: _____

_____

_____

My rating: _____

Cha Taqueria

● ● ● ● ● ● ● ● ● ● ● ● ● ● ● ● ● ● ●

NW/Nob Hill Map
305 NW 21st Ave.
(503) 295-4077
www.chaportland.com

Happy Hours
4:00–6:00pm Mon–Thur; 3:00–6:00pm Fri–Sun
10:00pm–midnight Fri–Sat

Food Deals 3+
$5.00
Unusual, gourmet *(delicioso!)* Mexican specialties
you'll need to see full descriptions for, but there's
a wide array and they are truly exceptional!

Drink Specials 3
$3.50 beer; $5.50 wine
$5.50 sangria; $5.50 margarita of the day

Atmosphere 3
Same owners as Cha Cha Cha, but Nob Hill's
version is more refined and elegant overall.
Big open space with cool, artsy white divider
and rough, lofty touches. Fun outside patio!

Date visited:

Went with:

Notes:

My rating:

Fonda Rosa

Lloyd Center-ish Map
108 NE 28th Ave.
(503) 235-3828

Happy Hours
4:00–6:00pm Tues–Sun

Food Deals 3
$3.00–$5.00
Solid neighborhood fave! Spinach w/goat cheese tlacoyos, ceviche or veggie tostadas, and tasty tacos with chicken, meat or salmon.

Drink Specials 3
$3.00 drafts; $5.00 wine selections;
$5.00 Margarita, $5.00 sangria or cosmo

Atmosphere 2
Simple in style with two bars; the narrow room is flanked by windows along 28th for lots of light and has a diner/coffeeshop feel by day, lounge by night.

Date visited: _____

Went with: _____

Notes: _____

_____

_____

My rating: _____

Isabel

●●●●●●●●●●●●●●●●●●●●●●

Pearl Map
330 NW 10th
(503) 222-4333
www.isabelscantina.com

Happy Hours
4:30–6:30pm Tues–Fri

Food Deals 3
$2.00 off all appetizers
Isabel's Cantina cookbook features "bold Latin flavors from the New California kitchen", as does her Happy Hour food: mini-carnitas tacos, steak bites, grilled shrimp, tofu, and rice bowls (carnitas, chicken & black bean or chicken & coconut).

Drink Specials 3
$4.00 beer; $4.00 wines; $5.00 sangria
$5.00 margaritas and specialty cocktails

Atmosphere 2
Located inside a small fishbowl-ish building of window walls; minimalist interior in need of some art or something/anything. Outdoor patio.

Date visited: _____

Went with: _____

Notes: _____

_____

_____

My rating: _____

ESPAÑOL(Mexican)

La Calaca Comelona

• • • • • • • • • • • • • • • • • • • •

Southeast Map
2304 SE Belmont
(503) 239-9675
www.lacalacacomelona.com

Happy Hours
8:00pm–close Mon–Sat★

Food Deals 3
$1.00–$6.00
Authentic, truly delicious Mexican food! Pork
and pineapple tacos (plus other varieties);
grilled cactus, spicy potatoes, mini quesadillas,
taquitos—and grilled grasshoppers!

Drink Specials 3
Varied and rotating menu

Atmosphere 3+
Take a Mexican vacation to this Day-of-the
Dead-inspired taverna named "The Hungry
Skeleton." Bright colorful walls, Mexican-style
folk art at every glimpse and turn, plus a
delightful beer garden (no Happy Hour seating).

Date visited: ....

Went with: ....

Notes: ....

....

....

My rating: ....

Limo

• • • • • • • • • • • • • • • •

TOP TEN FAVORITE!

NW/Nob HillMap
2340 NW Westover
(503) 477-8348
www.limorestaurant.com

Happy Hours
5:00–6:30 Tuesday–Friday

Food Deals 3+
$4.00–$8.00
Ceviche lovers rejoice! Many varieties of ceviche
offered (like classic, creamy, mixed seafood,
Asian and mushroom styles) with every one
of 15 or so appetizers half-off. Also enjoy soup,
corn pudding, skewers, potatoes with trio of
sauces, mussels. (OMG! This food is so good!!)

Drink Specials 2
$1.00 off beer, wine and delicious sangria

Atmosphere 3
Limo (LEE-mo) is located in a beautiful old
home/mansion, just one tree-lined block away
from trendy-third. Cozy, warm and homey, yet
sophisticated for fine dining. Cute outside patio.

Date visited: _____

Went with: _____

Notes: _____

_____

_____

My rating: _____

Lolo

● ●

Alberta Map
2940 NE Alberta St
(503) 288-3400
www.lolopdx.com

Happy Hours
4:30–6:30 Tuesday–Friday

Food Deals 2
$2.00–$7.00
Unique Spanish nibbles like rustic bread plate,
toasted almonds and marinated olives; or tapas
including papas bravas, spiced chicken skewers,
and pickled sardines; salad and cheeseburgers.

Drink Specials 3
$3.00 beer; $5.00 house wines; $5.00 sangria
$5.00 bartender's choice cocktail

Atmosphere 2
Upscale tapas bar; big open room with floor-to-
ceiling windows along Alberta Street; simple
style with neutral tones and chalkboard menus.

Date visited: ....

Went with: ....

Notes: ....

....

....

My rating: ....

Oba!

TOP TEN FAVORITE!

Pearl Map
555 NW 12th Ave.
(503) 228-6161
www.obarestaurant.com

Happy Hours
4:00–6:30pm Mon–Sat
9:30pm–close Mon–Thurs
4:00pm–close Sundays★

Food Deals 3
$4.50–$7.00
Many muy delicioso items! Queso fundito, green
chile mac & cheese, Puerto Rican fried rice,
grilled Baja chicken tacos, burgers, fritters.

Drink Specials 3
$4.00 selected beer; $5.00 house wine
$5.00 Margaritas; $4.75 cosmo or lemondrop

Atmosphere 3
Colorful, Latin American style with a festive and
trendy scene; outdoor sidewalk dining. "The kind
of place you need to hit *before* confession."

Date visited: _____

Went with: _____

Notes: _____

_____

_____

My rating: _____

Pambiche

Lloyd Center-ish Map
2811 NE Glisan
(503) 233-0511
www.pambiche.com

Happy Hours
★2:00–6:00pm Mon–Fri; 10:00pm–mid Fri–Sat

Food Deals 3
$2.50–$4.00
Mmmmpenadas, fried plantains, salads, bean and rice dishes, fried chicken and pork, shredded beef, stew—and don't miss the desserts!

Drink Specials 3
$3.00 Peruvian Cristal beer
$4.00 house red and white wines
$5.00 red and white sangrias
$1.50–$3.00 espressos, sodas, juices & shakes

Atmosphere 3
Fun and colorful Cuban café! Outdoor dining area streetside, bright, cozy and happy inside; vibrant exterior. Captures the Cuban "feel" well.

Date visited: _____

Went with: _____

Notes: _____

_____

_____

My rating: _____

Patanegra

8

1818 NW 23rd Place
(503) 227-7282
www.patanegra-restaurant.com

Happy Hours
4:00-6:00pm Tues–Fri

Food Deals 3
$5.00
Unique Spanish tapas-style small plates served in authentic, terra-cotta dishware with plenty to share: empanadas, calamari, stews, croquetas.

Drink Specials 1
$5.00 Spanish house wine and sangria

Atmosphere 3
Warm and welcoming with faux-painted orange walls. Giant rustic farmhouse exposed beams overhead, open working kitchen, and colorful, original artwork.

Date visited: _____

Went with: _____

Notes: _____

_____

_____

My rating: _____

Trébol

• •

Northeast/Mississippi Map
4835 N Albina Ave
(503) 517-9347
www.trebolpdx.com

Happy Hours
5:00-6:30pm and 9:00pm–close Daily

Food Deals 3
$2.00–$6.00
Authentic and interesting Mexican dishes with
soup to nuts, enchiladas, tacos, pork sandwich,
quesadilla, flautas (all fancier than they sound).

Drink Specials 2
$5.00 wines and sangrias (red or white)
$6.00 specialty margaritas: $5.00 mimosas
(plus a menu of 70+ tequilas)

Atmosphere 3
Perfect balance of modern and traditional style
with rustic wood tables, exposed rafters and
vents, gold and orange walls with framed prints,
huge illuminated bar and cool curtain dividers.

Date visited: _____

Went with: _____

Notes: _____

_____

_____

My rating: _____

FRENCH

Brasserie Montmarte

9

626 SW Park Avenue
(503) 236-3036
www.brasserieportland.com

Happy Hours
3:00-6:00pm and 9:00–11:00pm Daily

Food Deals 3
$3.00–$5.00
Limited, but delicious menu includes pommes frites, crispy artichoke hearts, mac & cheese, baked brie, and one of the best burgers in town!

Drink Specials 2
$5.00 house wine; $5.00 cocktail of the day

Atmosphere 3
To city-wide delight – the legend has reappeared! It really is a beautifully done space with black and white checkerboard floors, giant gilded-gold mirrors, and yes – award-winning crayon art.

Date visited: _____
Went with: _____
Notes: _____
_____
_____

My rating: _____

Café Reese

● ●

NW/Nob Hill Map
1037 NW 23rd Ave
(503) 219-0633
www.cafereese.com

Happy Hours
4:30–6:30pm Daily

Food Deals 3
$3.00–$5.00
Wide mix of food with wide range of international
influences: pommes frites, patatas bravas, soup,
calamari, several pizzettas, burgers, dolmas.

Drink Specials 3
$2.50 draft beer; $4.00 wines
$5.00 wells; $5.50 cocktail of the day

Atmosphere 3
Big, coffeehouse-style with modern touches on
old French flea market style. Chalkboard menus,
leather bar stools, white brick, and distressed-
wood tables. Currently more of a French look,
headed for Mediterranean influences to match
diverse European menu. Remodeling soon.

Date visited: ....

Went with: ....

Notes: ....

....

....

My rating: ....

Carafe

10

Downtown (East)
200 SW Market St.
(503) 248-0004
www.carafebistro.com

Happy Hours
3:00–6:00pm Mon–Fri
(until 5:00pm Keller event nights)

Food Deals 3
$1.95–3.95
Wide range of mostly French-focused fare:
pommes frites, baguettes, salads, mussels,
croque monsieur, smoked salmon, crepes.

Drink Specials 3
$3.00 beer; $4.00 array of apertifs;
$4.00 French style cocktails;
$4.25–$5.50 mini-carafes of wine (cute!!)

Atmosphere 3
Sweet French bistro with buttery French-vanilla
walls; café tables and chairs, dark trim with
books and bric-à-brac; outdoor patio seating.

Date visited: _____

Went with: _____

Notes: _____

_____

_____

My rating: _____

Chez Joly

Old Town Map
135 NW Broadway
(503) 200-5544
www.chezjoly.com

Happy Hours
4:00–6:00pm Tues–Sat

Food Deals 2
$4.00–$8.00
Most importantly, they have the best fries in town!
French and fresh menu items like salads, ham
and cheese or veggie baguettes, mussels, and of
course, French onion soup and a cheese plate.

Drink Specials 2
$5.00 red or white wine; $1.00 off cocktails

Atmosphere 3
French and fresh, ultra-charming Parisian café
with high ceilings and buttercream walls. Sweet
charm continues with lace café curtains, toile
upholstered chairs, dark woods, light sconces,
and an impressively ginormous mirrror.

Date visited: _____

Went with: _____

Notes: _____

_____

_____

My rating: _____

FRENCH

Fenouil

• • • • • • • • • • • • • • • • • • •

TOP TEN FAVORITE!

Pearl Map
900 NW 11th Ave
(503) 525-2225
www.fenouilinthepearl.com

Happy Hours
4:00–6:00pm Daily

Food Deals 3
$3.00–$10.00
Half-off their extensive bistro menu (20 items)
includes salads, cheese plates, foie gras, salmon
w/spinach, oysters, mussels, burger, pommes
frites, and the best French onion soup ever!

Drink Specials 3
$2.00 off all beer; $5.00 wine selections
$5.00 cocktail or spirit special

Atmosphere 3+
Fenouil is truly someplace special. Completely
stunning upon entrance with glamorous, trés
ritzy style. Outside patio can't be beat either!
Pronounced fen-EW-eee (French for fennel).

Date visited: _____
Went with: _____
Notes: _____
_____
_____

My rating: _____

Gustav's

7★

• •

Several Locations:
5035 NE Sandy Blvd. (503) 288-5503
12605 SE 97th Ave. (503) 653-1391
10350 SW Greenburg Rd, Tigard (503) 639-4544
1705 SE 164th Ave, Vancouver (360) 883-0222
www.gustavs.net

Happy Hours
3:00–6:00pm and 9:00pm–close

Food Deals 3
$1.99–$4.99
A large array of German specialties and other hardy, old stand-bys: reuben or sheperd's pie, fish & chips, burgers, schnitzel strips, chicken skewers, swiss fondue, sliders, potato pancakes.

Drink Specials 0
Only Vancouver offers drink discounts

Atmosphere 3
With some imagination and a couple beers from the strong and authentic European tap line-ups, you too, can be transported to a genuine Bavarian bierstube. Gold star for pushing the concept.

Date visited: _____

Went with: _____

Notes: _____

_____

_____

My rating: _____

East India Company

●●●●●●●●●●●●●●●●●●●●●●●

Downtown (West) Map
821 SW 11th Ave
(503) 227-8815
www.eastindiacopdx.com

Happy Hours
4:00–7:00pm Mon–Sat

Food Deals 2
$3.00
Rare Indian Happy Hour food. Only five menu
items, but perfect to order one of each when
sharing: eggplant dip, fish fingerlings, wings,
veggie fritters with chutney, potato croquettes.

Drink Specials 1
$1.00 off all drinks; $7.00 cocktails

Atmosphere 2
Bar area is a bit stark and almost like eating
in a hallway. Nice enough overall, but the front
bar decor and ambiance pales in comparison to
the dark, rich, romantic restaurant in back. Not
set up well for more than three people.

Date visited: ....

Went with: ....

Notes: ....

....

....

My rating: ....

Mayura

• •

8

1323 NW 23rd Ave.
(503) 208-2259

Happy Hours
4:00-6:00 pm Mon-Fri

Food Deals 3
$2.00–$5.00
Several dishes fried in a home-made batter with
nice presentations: veggie samosas, masala
papad, spinach fritters, fried jalapenos, sautéed
cauliflower gobi or chicken with green chilis.

Drink Specials 1
$3.00 Kingfisher beer; $3.00 wells

Atmosphere 3
Refined, but not too elegant; nice and mellow.
Large room with four dining areas and most
peaceful after dark with mood lighting, white
linens, dark woods, jazz or indian music.

Date visited: _____
Went with: _____
Notes: _____
_____
_____

My rating: _____

Vindalho

....

SE Map
2038 SE Clinton
(503) 467-4550
www.vindalho.com

8

Happy Hours
5:00–6:00pm Tues–Sun

Food Deals 2
$5.00
Five choices that rotate somewhat based on seasonal ingredients plus an array of condiments and naan. Items like spicy lamb meatballs with tomato-yogurt curry, wings or pumpkin samosas.

Drink Specials 2
$3.50 draft beer; $6.00 wine; $4.00 wells
$7.00 specialty cocktails

Atmosphere 3
Very cool and contemporary architecture defies convention and expected southeast hash house decor, and bears few signs of old, traditional India. Sadly, Happy Hour is confined to the bar.

Date visited: ....
Went with: ....
Notes: ....
....
....

My rating: ....

County Cork

North/NE Map
1329 NE Fremont
(503) 284-4805

Happy Hours
4:00–6:00pm Mon–Fri

Food Deals 3
$2.00–$4.00
Good and big meal offerings: fish and chips, fries, Guinness stew, bangers & mash, and shepherd's pie with side salads, turkey wrap, burger, wings.

Drink Specials 2
$1.00 off drafts ($3.50 most pints—Imperial)
25 notable beers on a beautiful tap lineup

Atmosphere 2
Big, fun and colorful Irish pub; a welcoming, friendly shelter. Hand-painted tables, pub decor, bench seating, windows that open to the street, and sidewalk seating. Family friendly and some occasional live Irish music.

Date visited: _____

Went with: _____

Notes: _____

....

....

My rating: _____

Kell's Irish Pub

Old Town Map
112 SW 2nd Ave.
(503) 227-4057
www.kellsirish.com/portland

Happy Hours
4:00–7:00pm Mon–Fri; 7:00–10:00pm Sunday★
10:00pm–midnight Mon–Thurs

Food Deals 3
$3.00
Irish nachos, wings, Caesar, BLTC, burger or
sandwich with fries, quesadilla, oyster shooters,
sweet potato fries, and a Gorgonzola spread.

Drink Specials 0
Sadly, no drink specials

Atmosphere 3
You *know* a good time is to be had in this infamous
Portland Institution! Fun Irish vibe with crinkled
dollar bills covering the ceiling, a 40-foot bar,
and free Irish music Sunday 6:00–8:00pm.

Date visited: _____
Went with: _____
Notes: _____
_____
_____

My rating: _____

Paddy's

● ●

Downtown (East) Map
65 SW Yamhill
(503) 224-5626
www.paddys.com

Happy Hours
4:00–7:00pm and 10:00pm–2:00am Daily

Food Deals 2
$4.00–$6.00
Bar basics with some Irish thrown in: hummus,
beef, pork or corned beef sliders, nachos, wings,
poppers, calamari, shepard's pie.

Drink Specials 2
$3.50 Harp beer; $3.00 Bud; $4.00 wells.

Atmosphere 3
Under new ownership and brought up a level in
both fun and food factor. Warm, upscale Irish pub
with a heavenly wooden bar stacked sky-high
with spirits of all sorts; outdoor sidewalk seating.

Date visited: ....

Went with: ....

Notes: ....

....

....

My rating: ....

Bar Mingo

811 NW 21st Ave
(503) 445-4646
www.barmingonw.com

Happy Hours
4:00–6:00pm Daily

Food Deals 2
$5.00
Five for five: Something like salad, sausage plate, fried potatoes, grilled calamari or lamb meatballs.

Drink Specials 2
$5.00 beer (kind of... two PBRs)
$5.00 choice red or white wine
$5.00 daily cocktail or bellinis

Atmosphere 3
Big in size and style with modern Italian design and some groovy West Elm touches. Warm, harvest tones with giant chalkboard map of Italy. Several pillowy conversation pits. Outdoor sidewalk seating at HH.

Date visited: _____

Went with: _____

Notes: _____

_____

_____

My rating: _____

ITALIAN

Ciao Vito

● ● ● ● ● ● ● ● ● ● ● ● ● ● ● ● ●

Alberta Map
2203 NE Alberta
(503) 282-5522
www.ciaovito.net

Happy Hours
4:00–8:00pm Mon-Thurs★; 4:00–6:00pm Fri-Sat
★All night Sunday

Food Deals 3
$2.00–$6.00
Nice array of rotating Italian menu items: salads,
pastas, polenta, roasted beets, meatballs, soup,
frittata, or maybe a zucchini panini.

Drink Specials 3
$3.00 pints; $4.00 wines
$5.00 bartender specialty cocktail

Atmosphere 3
Classic elegance with warmth and style, nice
neighborhood welcoming feel with bright and
funky mural on outside side wall.

Date visited: _____

Went with: _____

Notes: _____

_____

_____

My rating: _____

Fratelli (Bar Dué)

●●●●●●●●●●●●●●●●●●●●●●●●●●●

Pearl Map
1230 NW Hoyt
(503) 241-8800
www.fratellicucina.com

Happy Hours
4:30–6:00pm and 9:00pm–close Daily

Food Deals 2
$5.00
Tasty pizzettes and small plates are only slightly discounted from regular prices: six styles of pizzettes (mostly veggie options); veal meatballs, panini, polenta, pasta, lasagna, mixed green salad.

Drink Specials 2
$5.00 red or white wine; $4.00 wells
$6.00 cello drops

Atmosphere 3
Narrow, long, loft space with super-high ceilings; rough concrete walls with spotlight on nice, large abstract art pieces; upholstered bench seating with lots of candlelit tables.

Date visited: ....

Went with: ....

Notes: ....

....

....

My rating: ....

Il Piatto

Southeast
2342 SE Ankeny
(503) 236-4997
www.ilpiattopdx.com

Happy Hours
5:30–6:30pm Daily

Food Deals 2
$3.00–$6.00
Mushroom crepes, sauteed portobellos, calamari, gnocchi, penne, crostini with white bean spread, Caesar and panzanella salads, and desserts.

Drink Specials 1
$5.00 red or white wine

Atmosphere 3+
Dripping with artsy, classic Italian character and one of the best interiors in Portland! Capture the spirit of sipping wine late-night in old Venice nestled in a couch pit or curtained table nook. The Jade Lounge is connected to it (page 251).

Date visited: _____

Went with: _____

Notes: _____

_____

_____

My rating: _____

Mama Mia Trattoria

Downtown (East) Map
439 SW 2nd Ave.
(503) 295-6464
www.mamamiatrattoria.com

Happy Hours
5:00–7:00pm Mon–Sat 11:00pm–midnight Fri&Sat
★All night Sunday

Food Deals 3
$3.00
Plentiful and delicious pasta dishes including
meatballs, pasta dishes, lasagna of-the-day,
manicotti, Caesar salad, minestrone, plus fried
calamari and zucchini.

Drink Specials 0
Sadly, no drink specials

Atmosphere 3
Mama mia! Now that's Italian! Dripping in old
world ambience with nearly 100 gilded mirrors,
20 chandeliers, red velvet, gold gilding, fancy
white tablecloths, and romantic candlelight.

Date visited: ....

Went with: ....

Notes: ....

....

....

My rating: ....

Pazzo Ristorante

9

• • • • • • • • • • • • • • • •

Downtown (East) Map
627 SW Washington
(503) 228-1515
www.pazzoristorante.com

Happy Hours
3:00–6:00pm Daily

Food Deals 2
$3.00–$6.00
Simple, mostly Italian-style bar eats: artisan cured meat plates, manicotti, verona salad, brick oven pizzas and mixed marinated olives.

Drink Specials 3
$3.00 pints; $4.00 house wines
$3.00 wells; $5.00 cocktails

Atmosphere 3
The PazzoBAR side of Pazzo's Ristorante is stately and traditional in tone, rather than countryside Italian. It hosts a low-key and popular after-work bar scene.

Date visited: _____

Went with: _____

Notes: _____

_____

_____

My rating: _____

Sal's Famous Italian

NW/Nob Hill Map
33 NW 23rd Place
(503) 467-4067
www.salskitchen.com

Happy Hours
3:30–5:30pm Daily

Food Deals 3
$5.00
Delicious samplings of all the most popular dishes:
steamed mussels, caprese or Caesar salad,
burgers, spaghetti, pizza, butternut squash ravioli.

Drink Specials 3
$3.00 beer; $5.00 house wine
$4.00 well drinks; $6.00 featured cocktails

Atmosphere 3
Hip *and* quaint old-world Italian trattoria with
gorgeous faux wall treatments and walls of
classic framed pictures. Sweet space inside, but
in strip mall.

Date visited: _____

Went with: _____

Notes: _____

_____

_____

My rating: _____

ITALIAN

Serratto

10

TOP TEN FAVORITE!

NW/Nob Hill Map
2112 NW Kearney
(503) 221-1195
www.serratto.com

Happy Hours
4:00–6:00pm Daily

Food Deals 3
$4.00–$6.00
13 stellar menu items: stone oven pizzas (YUM),
prawns, fries, rigatoni, flame-broiled burgers,
salads, calamari, hummus, mussels, soup.

Drink Specials 3
$3.00 drafts; $5.00 red or white house wine
$5.00 cocktail specials

Atmosphere 3
Happy Hour is in their more casual "Vineria"
which is only slightly Italian in ambience,
but extremely pleasant and even romantic.

Date visited: _____

Went with: _____

Notes: _____

_____

_____

My rating: _____

MEDITERRANEAN

Cypress

●●●●●●●●●●●●●●●●●●●●●●●

Waterfront Map
1811 SW River Dr.
(503) 222-2027
www.cypressrestaurantandbar.com

Happy Hours
3:00–6:00pm Daily

Food Deals 3
$2.50–$5.00
Full boat of mezas offered: hummus, tabouli,
baba ganoush, tzatziki, and falafel; salads, soup,
gyro, chicken (pita, rice bowl and coco curry).

Drink Specials 3
$3.50 draft beers; $4.00 well drinks
$5.00 red and white wine
$4.00 martinis and specialty cocktails galore

Atmosphere 2
Red brick and sand-textured walls start to
allude to the island way, and the gregarious
party-nature of the hosts bring it home. Best
service I've had in Portland! Outside dining.

Date visited: _____

Went with: _____

Notes: _____

_____

_____

My rating: _____

MEDITERRANEAN
Greek Cusina

● ●

Downtown (East) Map
404 SW Washington
(503) 224-2288
www.greekcusina.com

Happy Hours
3:00–7:00pm Mon–Thurs; 3:00–6:00pm Fri
All Day Sunday★

Food Deals 3
$1.95–3.95
Big, cheap menu includes Greek salad, calamari,
gyro bites, dip sampler, falafel with tahini, chicken
flatbread pizza, breaded tiger prawns, saganaki.

Drink Specials 3
$3.00 drafts or bottled beer; $3.00 wells
$4.00 house specialties

Atmosphere 2
Outside marked by landmark giant purple
octopus! Mediterranean decor and color scheme;
booths with big open windows and walls; fun
octopus lamps. Happy Hour in downstairs bar.

Date visited: _____

Went with: _____

Notes: _____

_____

_____

My rating: _____

Lauro Kitchen

Southeast Map
3377 SE Division
(503) 239-7000
www.laurokitchen.com

Happy Hours
5:00–6:00pm Mon–Sat

Food Deals 2
$5.00–$8.00
Lauro's Hour of Happiness takes the most popular
menu items and prices them at 2003 levels.
Three choices like pizza, burger or calamari.

Drink Specials 2
$3.50 micobrews; $4.00 red or white wine

Atmosphere 3
An especially nice and upscale refuge as a
foodie stand-out in the hipster-hippie hub of
southeast Portland. Earthy, natural tones with
comfy seating, lots of light, wall-sized chalkboard menus, and overhead boxy, red lights.

Date visited: ....

Went with: ....

Notes: ....

....

....

My rating: ....

Afrique Bistro (African)

North/NE Map 102 NE Russell St; (503) 943-6616
www.afriquebistro.com

Happy Hours 5:00–7:00pm Thur–Mon

Food Deals 3 $3.00 Half-off delicious, unique and
fresh menu: big salads, hot & spicy stuffed portobello
mushroom, grilled prawns or wings with sauces.

Drink Specials 2 $1.00 off beer, wine or wells

Atmosphere 2 Bright and new with high ceilings,
giant windows, comfy, cushioned chairs (all too rare!),
and a small collection of African art and music.

Aqui Mexican

North/NE Map 1408 SE 12th Ave.; (503) 230-9212

Happy Hours 5:00–6:00pm Mon–Wed;
4:00–6.00pm Thur–Fri; 3:00–6:00pm Sat

Food Deals 2 $1.50–$4.95 Simple range of the usual
but popular, Mexican eats like tacos, quesadillas,
nachos, chips and salsa or guac, Caesar salad, soup.

Drink Specials 2 $2.50 beer; $3.50 wells;
$4.50 Margaritas

Atmosphere 2 Can't always judge a book by its
cover – its shockingly cute inside! Authentic Mexican
taqueria that's quite cozy and very casual.

Bocci's on 7th (Italian)

Central Eastside Map 1728 SE 7th; (503) 234-1616

Happy Hours 3:00–6:00pm / 9:00pm–12:00am Wed–Sat

Food Deals 2 $2.50–$5.50 Fried polenta, Ceasar with
or w/o chicken, fries, pasta of the day, garlic bread.

Drink Specials 2 $1.50–$3.50 random drink specials

Atmosphere 1 Non-descript and small space without
any Italian coziness factors in sight. More like a blue
collar worker lunch diner.

Cha Cha Cha (Mexican)

NE Map 3808 N. Williams #124; (503) 281-1655

Happy Hours 3:00–6:00pm Daily

Food Deals 3 $3.00 Nice array of homemade Mexican: tostadas, fish tacos, quesadillas, tacos, soup, salads.

Drink Specials 2 $3.00 beer, sangrias, Margaritas

Atmosphere 2 Colorful, bright and fresh, warehouse-style restaurant in the HUB strip on Williams. It's just a bit charmed up with Mexican art – and lots of tequila!

Iorio (Italian) www.ioriorestaurant.com

SE Map 912 SE Hawthorne; (503) 445-4716

Happy Hours 5:00–6:00pm Tues

Food Deals 2 $6.00–$7.00 Big servings, but only four choices: pulled pork sandwich, risotto, pasta, burger.

Drink Specials 0 Sadly, no drink specials

Atmosphere 3 Big on red in big, open room with long, central family table and window seats. Low light, dark wood floors, and original paintings depicting country life in bright colors and ornate gold frames.

Por Que No (Mexican)

Mississippi Map 3524 N Mississippi; (503) 467-4149
Southeast Map 4635 SE Hawthorne; (503) 954-3138

Happy Hours 3:00–6:00pm Daily; Tues 3:00pm–close

Food Deals 1 $2.00 tacos; $1.00 off chips & guac or salsa. Cheap menu at all times; authentic Mexican.

Drink Specials 2 $2.50 bottled beer; $3.00 drafts $4.50 and $7.00 margaritas; $4.00 sangrias

Atmosphere 2 A true taqueria vibe, complete with loud music, warm colors, and noisy kitchen ramblings.

Porto Terra (Italian)

Downtown Map 830 SW 6th Ave.; (503) 944-1090
www.portoterra.com

Happy Hours 3:30–6:30pm Mon–Fri

Food Deals 2 $2.50–$7.00 Big Italian menu of pizza, bruschetta, antipasto, polenta, tortellini, meatball polpetta, mixed greens or Caesar salads, calamari.

Drink Specials 1 $5.00 house red or white wine

Atmosphere 3 Hilton hotel bar with Tuscan countryside modern motif; an upscale, contemporary slice of Italy.

Santa Fe (Mexican)

NW/Nob Hill Map 831 NW 23rd; (503) 220-0406
www.santafetaqueria.com

Happy Hours 4:00–7:00pm Daily

Food Deals 2 $2.50–$4.50 Big menu with lots of the basics: chicken, ground beef or mahi mahi tacos, wings, jalapeno poppers, nachos, prawns, ceviche.

Drink Specials 2 50 cents off beer; $5.00 wine $3.00 wells; $4.50 Margaritas

Atmosphere 1 A popular, neighborhood watering hole. Good for trivia and outdoor sidewalk seating.

Sushi Land (Marinepolis)

Pearl Map 138 NW 10th Ave; (503) 546-9933
www.sushilandusa.com

Happy Hours 4:00–7:00pm Daily

Food Deals 2 $1.50 Your choice of every kind of sushi sample under the sun! (23 nigiri and 27 rolls)

Drink Specials 3 $3 beer, $4 wine, $5 cocktails

Atmosphere 2 An upstairs bar awaits – eye-level with the black ceiling ductwork, you'll overlook the diner below. Simple, but nice enough at night.

Thai Noon (My Thai Lounge)

Alberta Map 2635 NE Alberta St.; (503) 282-2021
www.thainoon.com

Happy Hours 4:30–6:30pm Mon–Sat

Food Deals 2 $2.75–$7.00 Thai basics like egg rolls,
wontons, satay, fried rice, pad thai, padkeemoo.

Drink Specials 2 $3.00 beers; $2.00 PBRs;
$4.50 cocktails; $3.00 well drinks

Atmosphere 1 Super casual, somewhat spartan
lounge next to the Thai Noon restaurant.

Zaytoon (Mediterranean)

Alberta Map 2236 NE Alberta; (503) 284-1168
www.zaytoonbar.com

Happy Hours 5:00–7:00pm Daily
All night "Happy Mondays 2-3-4 deal"
($2.00 beer $3.00 well; $4.00 select wine)

Food Deals 2 $2.00–$8.00
Hummus, falafel, bamyia, olives, meatballs, laban, meza
platter, baba's burger; plus falafel, veggie wraps.

Drink Specials 2 $3.00 drafts; $1.00 PBR; $4.00 wells

Atmosphere 2 Minimalist, hi-tech, and artsy with huge
windows and soaring ceilings and long modern bar.

Zilla Saké (Sushi)

Alberta Map 1806 NE Alberta; (503) 336-4104
www.zillasakehouse.com

Happy Hours 5:00–7:00pm Daily

Food/Drink Sake Pairings 3 $1.00–$11.00 Must
love sake (and the resultant funbuzz...ahem)! Some
delicious sushi and such with savings on sake.

Atmosphere 2
Cool and artsy zen. *Huge* sake menu. Dramatic,
large-scale art and big screen TV with Japanese flicks.

Sports & Pool

Watch TV,
Drink a Beer,
Play Pool

There are admittedly a *lot* more sportsbars in town than are covered in the following pages, but I was focusing on some of the nicer places, close-in, and ones that have good Happy Hours.

On the pool side, there are literally hundreds of bars in town to play pool, so I'm hardly scratching the surface here.

Some other places listed in this book with pool tables include Buffalo Gap, Goodfoot (four tables upstairs), Henry's (big top floor pool room), Hopworks Urban Brewery, Life of Riley, and Mashtun. Also, most McMenamin's have pool tables, most especially their "Tavern & Pool" place on 23rd.

The Agency

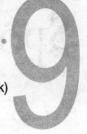

1939 SW Morrison (next to PGE Park)
(503) 548-2921
www.theagencyentertainment.com

Happy Hours
3:00–6:00pm Mon–Fri (food & drinks)
10:00pm–2:00am Thur–Sat (food only)

Food Deals 3
$3.00–$4.00
Sporty bar menu with spins on basics: cheeseburger, bacon cheddar fries, sushi rolls, won ton
nachos, BBQ riblets, wings, pork slider.

Drink Specials 2
$2.00 PBR; $2.50 Buds; 3.00 Miller; $3.50 micro
$4.00 flavored stoli vodka drinks

Atmosphere 3
Happy Hour is in the bar area of this "ultra sport
lounge." Very sleek and almost night-clubby
look and feel. Watch your favorite teams on the
tower of 12 TVs or one of many over the bar.

Date visited: _____

Went with: _____

Notes: _____

_____

_____

My rating: _____

Blitz Ladd

Southeast (off map)
2239 SE 11th Ave
(503) 236-3592
www.blitzpdx.com

Happy Hours
3:00-6:00pm Mon-Fri; 11:00pm-close (food) Daily

Food Deals 2
$3.00–$6.25
About a dozen bar menu items like quesadillas, sliders, salads, pizza, quesadillas, burgers, salads, chicken fingers, hummus and... totchos!

Drink Specials 2
50 cents off beer ($2.50–$3.50)
$5.00 house wines; $3.00 wells

Atmosphere 3
Huge room with several different seating areas. *Plenty* of hi-def TVs (including 15 52" screens plus a 12 ft. giant projection screen). Done up in natural woods with plenty of tables and couches too. Pool, shuffleboard and ping pong tables.

Date visited: ....

Went with: ....

Notes: ....
....
....

My rating: ....

Blitz Pearl

●●●●●●●●●●●●●●●●●●●●●●●

8

Pearl Map
110 NW 10th Ave
(503) 222-2229
www.blitzpdx.com

Happy Hours
3:00–7:00pm Daily

Food Deals 2
$1.00–$4.00
15 basic bar standards like quesadillas, sliders,
Caesar salad, chicken fingers, pretzels, cookies,
hummus and YAY! They've got totchos!

Drink Specials 3
$2.00 domestic beers; $3.00 microbrews
$5.00 house wines; $3.00 wells

Atmosphere 2
Sporty, designed-on-a-dime collegiate feel with
light, beaded-board plank paneling and heavily
varnished particle board tables. Game rooms.
Tables and booths surrounding one big central
bar, so not the best TV viewage. Outdoor seating.
New "Blitz Buzz" coffee shop upstairs (7:00am).

Date visited: _____

Went with: _____

Notes: _____

_____

_____

My rating: _____

Buffalo Wild Wings

●●●●●●●●●●●●●●●●●●●●●●●●●●●

8

Downtown (West) Map
327 SW Morrison; (503) 224-1309
www.buffalowildwings.com

<u>Hillsboro:</u> 2219 NW Allie; (503) 645-9424
<u>Cascade Station</u>:
9810 NE Cascades Parkway (503) 281-0351

Happy Hours
3:00–6:00pm Mon–Fri

Food Deals 2
$2.00–$4.50
Greasy bar food that's oh-so-delicious: basket
of fries, onion rings or mozzarella stix; chili con
queso, nachos, cheeseburger, popcorn shrimp.
Go for 50 cent wing nights Tuesday & Thursday.

Drink Specials 3
$1.00 off beer (decent line-up of microbrews)
$2.50 wells, $3.00 Margarita, lemondrop or cosmo

Atmosphere 2
Sporty, collegiate atmosphere that's good
clean fun for everyone; hi-def TVs *everywhere*.

Date visited: _____

Went with: _____

Notes: _____

_____

_____

My rating: _____

Grand Central Bowl

• •

6

Central Eastside Map
839 SE Morrison
503.236.BOWL (2695)
www.thegrandcentralbowl.com

Happy Hours
3:00–6:30pm Mon–Fri;
10:00pm–1:00am Sun–Thurs

Food Deals 2
$2.50–$4.95
Nice and cheap line-up of bar basics like sliders,
fries, artichoke dip, onion rings, lettuce wraps,
cheese sticks, spicy tuna rolls and pizzas.

Drink Specials 0
Sadly, no drink specials

Atmosphere 3
A $14-million renovation brings a flashy, fancy-
smancy bowling mecca! It's a party place in a
giant space with several bars, lounges, game
rooms and plenty of hi-def, big-screen TVs.

Date visited: _____

Went with: _____

Notes: _____

_____

_____

My rating: _____

Macadams

Waterfront Map
5833 SW Macadam
(503) 246-6227
www.macadamsbarandgrill.com

Happy Hours
3:00–6:00pm Daily; 9:00pm–mid Mon–Thurs
★ All night Sunday (3:00–midnight)

Food Deals 3
$2.50–$5.00
Big bar menus includes pulled pork sliders,
cheeseburger, or chicken strips with fries; brat,
jalapeno-artichoke dip, Buffalo wrap, Caesar,
mac & cheese, BBQ chicken pizza, calamari.

Drink Specials 1 Rotating specials after 9pm

Atmosphere 3
Lofted lodge effect with traditional manly-man
tans and browns. Plenty of TVs for watching
your favorite games. Outdoor patio area. Family
friendly in restaurant until 8:00pm.

Date visited: _____

Went with: _____

Notes: _____

_____

_____

My rating: _____

Madison's

Southeast
1109 SE Madison
(503) 230-2471
www.madisonsgrill.com

Happy Hours
3:00–6:00pm and 10:00–close Daily (no late Sun)
$2.00 Tuesdays = 16 taps $2 microbrews all night

Food Deals 2
$3.00–$5.00
Hummus, quesadilla, wings, mound of nachos,
onion rings, salads, sliders, fish or shrimp tacos,
dips, and BBQ chicken skewers.

Drink Specials 2
Beers are 75 cents off
$3.75 well drinks; $4.00 select house wines

Atmosphere 2
Friendly, casual hang-out place; brass and fern
family style; outdoor wood deck available for
Happy Hour. Renovation and BBQ pros soon.
Limited TVs. Party space. Free pool!

Date visited: _____

Went with: _____

Notes: _____

_____

_____

My rating: _____

On Deck Sports

Pearl Map
910 NW 14th Ave.
(503) 227-7020
www.ondecksportsbar.com

Happy Hours
3:30–6:30pm Mon–Fri; 9:00pm–close Daily

Food Deals 2
$2.00–4.00
Bar food basics: nachos, salad, Caesar, chicken
strips, burgers w/fries, garlic fries, chips & salsa,
pulled pork sliders and "the hummus among us."

Drink Specials 2
$3.75 micros; $2.75 domestics; $5.00 wines
$2.50 wells!

Atmosphere 3
Really as nice as a sports bar can be: red-brick-
colored walls and wall-to-wall windows; hi-tech
wavy black ceiling tiles; hi-def TVs surrounding
the rounded bar in middle. Huge deck gets better
and better as the night gets darker and darker.

Date visited: _____

Went with: _____

Notes: _____

_____

_____

My rating: _____

Rialto

Downtown (East) Map
529 SW 4th Ave.; (503) 228-7605
Tigard: 14411 SW Pacific Hwy; (503) 620 6633
www.rialtopoolroom.com

Happy Hours
4:00–7:00pm Mon–Fri; 11:00pm–close Sun–Thur

Food Deals 2
$3.00–$5.00
Bar eats like grilled chicken skewers, chicken strips, grilled cheese & tomato soup, tacos.

Drink Specials 2
$2.00–3.00 micros $2.00 wells!

Atmosphere 2
Large, open, and bright pool room with tables in good condition; casual in tone; also has snooker, off-track betting, and pinball. Sports watching scene? Not so much.

Date visited: _____

Went with: _____

Notes: _____

_____

_____

My rating: _____

Thirsty Lion Pub

Old Town Map
71 SW 2nd Ave.
(503) 222-2155
www.thirstylionpub.com

Happy Hours
3:00-7:00pm Mon–Fri; 10:00pm-close Sun–Thur

Food Deals 2
$2.95–$4.95
Ten or so pretty basic, but good, bar menu items
like fish or pork sliders, giant pretzels, mozzarella
sticks, salads, nachos, calamari, brats, fries.

Drink Specials 2
$2.50 domestics; $3.50 microbrews; $3.25 wells

Atmosphere 2
A touch more sterile version of a neighborhood
English Pub, being more yuppie and huge. Food,
spirits, ales, live music, sports on several TVs.

Date visited: _____

Went with: _____

Notes: _____

_____

_____

My rating: _____

Touché

• •

Pearl Map
1425 NW Glisan
(503) 221-1150
www.touchepdx.com

Happy Hours
4:00-6:30pm Daily; All day Sun (4:00pm-2:30am)

Food Deals 2
$3.00 gyros (chicken, lamb or veggie), $4.00 pizzas & Caesar, $5.00 Mediterranean platter.

Drink Specials 2
$2.00 Miller beers; $3.00 microbrews; $3.00 wells

Atmosphere 2
Semi-stately pool hall with grand staircase entrance and six nice full-size tables. Great for both stylish pool boys and true sharks. Keep the restaurant downstairs in mind for a real meal! More for pool as opposed to great sports viewing.

Date visited: _____

Went with: _____

Notes: _____

_____

_____

My rating: _____

Waterfront

On the Water

Columbia River

Willamette River

Sandy River

Lake Oswego

There's something about drinking near water that makes life happier! We're blessed here in Portland to have a number of different options at water's edge, each with a totally different vantage point. *This* is a section worthy of many repeat visits!

Aquariva

●●●●●●●●●●●●●●●●●●●●●●

Willamette River (South)
0470 SW Hamilton Ct
(503) 802-5850
www.aquarivaportland.com

Happy Hours
2:30–6:30pm and 9:30pm–close Daily

Food Deals 3
$1.00–$5.00
Somewhat Italian-inspired menu mixed with
seasonal fresh NW influences: veal and pork
meatballs, fries, fritters, grilled veggies, oysters.

Drink Specials 2
$3.00 select beer; $5.00 wine
$20 bottles of wine; $5.00 bellinis

Atmosphere 3
Totally striking architecture and design delights
and captivates upon entrance and draws you in
wanting more – resplendent river views await!
Ultra-contemporary with comfy couch pits, cocktail
tables and soaring ceilings. Outside patio too.

Date visited: ....

Went with: ....

Notes: ....

....

....

My rating: ....

Beaches

• • • • • • • • • • • • • • • • • • •

8

Columbia River (Vancouver)
1919 SE Columbia River Dr.
(360) 699-1592
www.beachesrestaurantandbar.com

Happy Hours
3:00–6:00pm Daily
9:00–11:00pm Tues–Sat
9:00–10:00pm Sun–Mon

Food Deals 2
$1.95-$5.95
Huge menu with several pizza and salad choices, burger, ribs, salmon, sesame pork, wings, soups, taters, shrimp quesadilla, and nightly dessert fix.

Drink Specials 2
$3.50 beer; $3.95 nightly cocktail special

Atmosphere 3
SO nice along the river here, but Happy Hour is in the inside bar area only. Overall, has a fun, but refined beach bar motif, wall-to-wall giant windows for river peeks and big stone fireplace.

Date visited: ....

Went with: ....

Notes: ....

....

....

My rating: ....

Five Spice

315 First St., Ste 201
(503) 697-8889
www.fivespicerestaurant.com ·······················

BEST OF LAKE OSWEGO

Happy Hours
3:00–6:00pm Mon-Fri

Food Deals 3
$5.00
Seasonal favorites vary slightly with items like
oysters on the half-shell, soup, fried squid, crab
cakes, field greens, plus bar menu of faves.
(Sign up for their mailing list for special offers).

Drink Specials 3
$5.00 selection of wines, cocktails and micro-
brews; plus 1/2 off bottles wine on Sundays

Atmosphere 3
Head upstairs to their lounge area for Happy
Hour and sit outside if possible for views of the
lake! Inside, it's pleasant as well, with Northwest
natural stylings, lots of light and huge windows.

Date visited: _____

Went with: _____

Notes: _____

_____

_____

My rating: _____

McCormick & Schmick's

Harborside Pilsner Room

Willamette River
0309 SW Montgomery
(503) 220-1865
www.mccormickandschmicks.com

Happy Hours
3:00–6:00pm and 9:00pm–close Daily

Food Deals 3
$1.95–4.95
Huge menu of about 20 or so items like prawns, scallops, or crab cakes, but then you almost always *have* to get the famous cheeseburger and fries for only $2.95!

Drink Specials 0
No drink specials at this location, but they have an exceptional NW tap line-up and are also a satellite facility of Hood River's Full Sail plant.

Atmosphere 3
Gorgeous and stately restaurant overlooking the Willamette River! Impressive, traditional-style. Happy Hour inside, on bar-side. Classy, but fun.

Date visited: _____

Went with: _____

Notes: _____

_____

_____

My rating: _____

Newport Seafood Grill

• •

9

Willamette River
0425 SW Montgomery
(503) 227-3474
www.newportbay.com

Happy Hours
3:00–6:00pm Daily
9:00–10:00pm Sun–Thu; 10:00–11:00pm Fri–Sat
Closed to public for winter season (Nov-Feb)

Food Deals 3
$3.00–$5.00
Big, cheap and delicious menu and servings:
fish & chips, cheddar burger, pear salad, chowder,
Caesar, calamari, shrimp cocktail, clams, dips.

Drink Specials 3
$3.50 draft beer, wines and well drinks

Atmosphere 3
Formerly known as Marina Fish House, located
right out over the river amidst the yachts, docks
and ducks in the marina. This is one of the best
places in Portland to kiss!

Date visited: _____

Went with: _____

Notes: _____

_____

_____

My rating: _____

Oswego Lake House

Lake Oswego (Lake Oswego Map)
40 N. State Street
(503) 636-4561
www.oswegolakehouse.com

Happy Hours
4:00–6:00pm Daily and 9:00pm–close Daily

Food Deals 3
$3.00–$6.00
They are finally getting it right with a great mix:
mac & cheese, soup, quesadilla, burgers, wings,
coconut shrimp, filet tips, prime rib sandwich.

Drink Specials 3
$3.00 draft beers; $5.00 house wines
$4.00 wells or martini

Atmosphere 2
Right on the lake with a stellar back deck area,
but that's not always (i.e. rarely) available for
Happy Hour goers. It's really dark inside this
somewhat nautical, traditional, old-school bar.

Date visited: _____

Went with: _____

Notes: _____

_____

_____

My rating: _____

Red Lion Quay

Columbia River (Vancouver)
100 Columbia St.
(360) 750-4940

Happy Hours
4:00–7:00pm Daily; 9:00pm–close Sun–Thurs

Food Deals 3
$3.00–$5.00
Lots to choose from – plentiful and cheap! Wings, calamari, burger, soup, salad, quesadilla, nachos, shrimp, clams, loaded baked potato, salads.

Drink Specials 2
$2.00 Coors, $5.00 house wines, $4.00 wells

Atmosphere 3
Houseboat-like interior with dark, oak wood everywhere, huge sailboat pulleys and thick ropes. River views, but more industrial looking as the I-5 bridge blocks things a bit.

Date visited: _____

Went with: _____

Notes: _____

_____

_____

My rating: _____

Riverview

Sandy River (off map)
29311 SE Stark, Troutdale
(503) 661-FOOD (3663)
www.yoshidariverview.com

Happy Hours
4:30–6:30pm Sun–Thurs

Food Deals 3
$2.00–$5.00
Nice mix of bar menu faves done well: calamari, fried butternut ravioli, sliders, salads, soup, spicy mac & cheese, mushroom bruschetta, won tons.

Drink Specials 3
$3.00 beer; $5.00 wine; $4.00 wells and cocktails

Atmosphere 3+
An absolutely gorgeous place! Fine dining with views of the Sandy River and surrounding forest. Happy Hour's bar area offers outdoor tables and is a perfect choice to hit after a Sunday Gorge hike (unless your shoes are muddy 'cause it's fancy here)! Frequent live music.

Date visited: _____

Went with: _____

Notes: _____

_____

_____

My rating: _____

Salty's

TOP TEN FAVORITE!

Columbia River
3839 NE Marine Drive
(503) 288-4444
www.saltys.com

Happy Hours
★4:00–6:00pm Mon–Fri;
4:30pm to close Sunday★

Food Deals 3
$1.50–$6.99
15 superb menu items including blackened salmon
or twisted Caesar, ribs, fish and chips, crab &
artichoke dip, coconut prawns, tuna melt, fries,
seafood chowder (yum!) and burgers (best!).

Drink Specials 3
$3.95 choice draft; $5.00 wine selections
$4.25 Margaritas & Bloody Marys

Atmosphere 3
Fine-dining waterside restaurant; wall-to-wall
giant windows and outdoor deck; yacht club
motif. *Gorgeous* scenery along the river, and
a great place to watch the sunset!

Date visited: _____

Went with: _____

Notes: _____

_____

_____

My rating: _____

Shenanigans

• •

7

Columbia River
909 N Hayden Island Drive
(503) 283-4466
www.shenanigansrestaurant.com

Happy Hours
4:00–7:00pm Mon–Thurs; 4:00–8:00pm Fridays

Food Deals 2
$1.95–$3.95
Parmesan calamari, salmon cakes, wings, rings,
fries, poppers, oyster shooters, burger, spring rolls.

Drink Specials 2
$3.75 drafts; $4.25 house wines; $4.25 wells

Atmosphere 3
Highest rating due to beautiful view along the
Columbia. Inside, their "Tuxedo Charley's" bar
has a large-screen, hi-def TV in the lounge area
with movie posters encircling the modern-day,
'70s Vegas-style hotel bar.

Date visited: _____

Went with: _____

Notes: _____

_____

_____

My rating: _____

Thirst

Willamette River
0315 SW Montgomery (RiverPlace)
(503) 295-2747
www.thirstwinebar.com

Happy Hours
3:00–6:00pm Tues–Fri
9:00pm–close Tues–Sun (food)

Food Deals 2
$2.00–$6.00
Nibbles perfect with wine and served with bread:
artisan cheese, olives, charcuterie plate, olive
tapenade, salad, gnocchi.

Drink Specials 3
$2.50 beer; $5.00 select wine; $2.00 tastes(!)

Atmosphere 3
Right on RiverPlace Esplanade with huge windows
and sidewalk seating for people and river gazing;
couch lounge area with fireplace. A truly enjoyable
wine bar! Check website for special events.

Date visited: _____

Went with: _____

Notes: _____

_____

_____

My rating: _____

Three Degrees

Willamette River
1510 SW Harbor Way
(503) 295-6166
www.threedegreesrestaurant.com

Happy Hours
4:00–7:00pm Daily

Food Deals 3
$3.00–$8.00
Half-off selections from their full menu: grilled cheese, cheeseburger, sweet potato fries, fish & chips, hummus plate, rigatoni.

Drink Specials 2
$4.00 pints and glasses of select wine

Atmosphere 3
Three is the magic number here: 3 o'clock start time, $3 food specials and $3 drink deals, too. Romantic upscale perfection; river view with lots of windows, cushy seats, and a cozy fireplace. Free valet parking!

Date visited: _____

Went with: _____

Notes: _____

_____

_____

My rating: _____

Tippy Canoe

Sandy River (off map)
28242 E Historic Columbia Hwy.
(503) 492-2220
www.shirleysfood.com

Happy Hours
3:00–6:00pm and 9:00pm–close Daily

Food Deals 3
$2.95–$3.95
Over a dozen super cheap and tasty menu items:
BBQ beef or ham sandwich, jalapeno poppers,
wings, soup or salad, taquitos, potstickers, chips.

Drink Specials 1
Barely there 50 cents of drinks on weekdays only

Atmosphere 3
Also known as Shirley's Tippy Canoe Bar & Grill
on the Sandy River. Remodeled and re-opened
in early 2009, it still retains the look and feel of
a 1940's woodsy, riverside lodge. Enjoy the patio
out back in the summer! Perfect location and
vibe when coming back from a hike in the Gorge.

Date visited: _____

Went with: _____

Notes: _____

_____

_____

My rating: _____

Who Song & Larry's

9

Columbia River (Vancouver)
111 SE Columbia Way
(360) 695-1198

Happy Hours
4:00–8:00pm Mon–Fri

Food Deals 3
$2.65–$4.99 (half-off appetizers)
99 cent "Taco Tuesdays" (4:00pm–10:00pm)
Big menu with BIG portions: taquitos, quesadillas,
wings, guacka wacka mole, nachos supreme,
sopes and tacos. Americanized Mexican food,
but the price is right at Happy Hour.

Drink Specials 3
$3.00 domestics; $3.50 house chardonnay
$3.00 wells; $4.25 margaritas

Atmosphere 3
Re-vamped and downplayed fiesta bar area with
stucco walls, doorway arches, wood beams and
carved, painted booths. Seating on outside deck
with sweeping views of the Columbia River!

Date visited: _____

Went with: _____

Notes: _____

_____

_____

My rating: _____

The Deck   www.thedeck.bz

Columbia River   33rd & Marine Dr.; (503) 283-6444

Happy Hours 12:00-6:00pm Daily ★
Seasonal/Outdoor (mid-April – end of September)

Food Deals 2 $2.00-$5.00 Bar eats with emphasis
on seafarer's grub; shrimp, fish tacos, chili, nachos.

Drink Specials 2 $2.50 domestic beers; $3.50 wells
$6.00 blended margaritas, mojitos, daiquiris, coladas

Atmosphere 3 Floating deck *on* the river (you'll feel
it move)! Down the ramp from McCuddy's parking lot,
past the harbor boats, to a slice of PDX paradise.

Island Café   www.islandcafepdx.com

Hayden Island   250 NE Tomahawk.; (503) 283-0362

Happy Hours 3:00-6:00pm Mon-Fri
Seasonal/Outdoor (mid-April – end of September)

Food Deals 2 $2.00-$5.00 Basic and limited pub grub

Drink Specials 1 Occasional good beer specials

Atmosphere 3 Totally tropical! Well, as much as you
can get in Portland anyway. A favorite treasure that's
worth fighting horrific traffic heading north on I-5.

Sextant

Columbia River 4035 NE Marine Dr.; (503) 281-5944

Happy Hours All night specials

Food Deals 1 Changing – Dinner-of-the-Day

Drink Specials 2 Changing – $1.75 domestics and
$3.00 micros are common featured specials

Atmosphere 3 Prime-positioned outdoor deck right
on the Columbia River, with view marred by chain-
link fence. Inside is casual and only slightly nautical;
Prime sunset views!

Quick Shots

The following pages briefly list

mini-reviews

of places that are more casual bars

as opposed to nicer restaurants like the

listings in the rest of the book.

Please note: Most Friday and Saturday

late-night Happy Hours may start an

hour later than indicated, and don't

always include the drinks side of things.

21st Avenue Bar & Grill

NW/Nob Hill 721 NW 21st Ave; (503) 222-4121

Happy Hours 3:00–6:00pm Mon–Fri; All day Sun
9:30pm–12:30am Mon–Thur

Food Deals 2 $3.00 Tons of bar food cheapies like
mac & cheese, nachos, tots, salads, wings, spring rolls.

Drink Specials 2 $1.25 PBR; $2.50 micros and wells

Atmosphere 2 Dive bar without too much character,
but with a secret, surprisingly cute back patio area!

Aalto Lounge

Southeast Map 3356 SE Belmont (503) 235-6041

Happy Hours 5:00–7:00pm Daily Daily

Food Deals 3 $2.00–$5.00 Big *and* delicious
portions: steak, meatball, ham & cheese or grilled
veggie sandwiches; fresh greens or Caesar salad,
stuffed mushrooms, crostini.

Drink Specials 2 $3.00 IPA drafts; $3.00 wells

Atmosphere 2 Compelling and retro-y with artsy
vibe, subtle funkiness, loungy ambience. Check out
the back patio on a nice day.

Alberta Street Pub

Alberta Map 1036 NE Alberta; (503) 284-7665
www.myspace.com/albertastreetpub

Happy Hours 5:00–8:00pm Mon–Fri

Food Deals 3 $3.00 Basic but big: turkey sandwich,
Guinness beef stew, salad, nachos, BLT, veggie
melt.

Drink Specials 3 $1.00 PBRs; $2.50 micros
$2.75 wells; $2.75 selected wine

Atmosphere 2 Warm and inviting, dark Irish pub.
High-walled booths enable private conversation.

Alibi Tiki Lounge

North/NE Map 4024 N Interstate; (503) 287-5335

Happy Hours 3:00–7:00pm Daily; 9:00–11:00pm
Sun–Thurs; 11:00am–7:00pm Sat–Sun

Food Deals 2 $1.95–$2.95
Bar fare with island touches; taco quesadilla, dinner
salad, hot wings, soup, onion rings, BBQ burger.

Drink Specials 2 $2.50 tropicals (nightly specials)

Atmosphere 3 Top marks for over-the-top tacky
Tiki; bizarrely dark & divey; a unique Portland treasure.

Arista www.aristapdx.com

SE Map 3862 SE Hawthorne; (503) 235-3364

Happy Hours 4:00–6:30pm / 9:00pm–close Thur–Sat

Food Deals 2 $2.00–$5.00 Nice array of a little bit
of everything: gumbo, grilled pork & apple sandwich,
fries, cavatapi, skewered prawns, burgers, bruschetta.

Drink Specials 2 $3.00 drafts; $4.00–5.00 wines

Atmosphere 2 Tiny, posh and low-lit lounge with lots
of black and sexy red; marble columns, dark wood
floors, chandeliers. Wonderful patio out front! Erratic
and inconsistent schedule at press time (phone first).

Bella Faccia Pizzeria

Alberta Map 2934 NE Alberta St.; (503) 282-0600
www.bellafacciapizzeria.com

Happy Hours
4:00–6:00pm Mon–Fri; 3:00–5:00pm Sat–Sun

Food Deals 2 $1.75–$2.50 pizza slices
Huge salads could feed up to 4 people $8.00–$9.00

Drink Specials 1 $1.00 off pints

Atmosphere 2 Very casual pizza place with coffee-
house vibe; pleasant back patio and sidewalk seating.

Berbati's

Old Town Map 231 SW Ankeny; (503) 248-4579
www.berbati.com

Happy Hours 4:00–7:00pm Daily

Food Deals 2 Yummy $3.00 gyros! $1.00 off other menu items like fries, hummus and salad.

Drink Specials 2 $2.00 domestics; $3.00 microbrews

Atmosphere 2 Greek arches over doors, faux aged walls, funky Aladdin lamps, cool copper studded floor, and original artwork. Outdoor patio seating.

Blue Monk

Southeast Map 3341 SE Belmont; (503) 595-0575
www.thebluemonk.com

Happy Hours 5:00–7:00pm Daily (Upstairs);
6:30–8:00pm Daily (Downstairs)

Food Deals 2 $5.50 for nice variety: shrimp tacos, seared ahi carpaccio, bruschetta plate, coconut polenta, meatball and sausage subs.

Drink Specials 3 $3.00 for drafts; $3.00 wells $5.50 house wine; $4.50 specialty cocktails

Atmosphere 2 Happy Hour downstairs where blue theme continues with pool and cool tunes.

Buffalo Gap www.thebuffalogap.com

Waterfront Map 6835 SW Macadam; (503) 244-7111

Happy Hours 4:00–6:00pm & 10:00–midnight Daily

Food Deals 2 $2.95 Basic bar standards

Drink Specials 1
A couple of random specials mostly for game nights.

Atmosphere 2
Reminiscent of a small-town tourist pub; meandering rooms with some farm-style touches; TVs/sports.

Camellia Lounge www.teazone.com

Pearl Map 510 NW 11th Ave.; (503) 221-2130

Happy Hours 4:00–7:00pm Daily; All Sun (10–8pm)

Food Deals 2 $2.00–$5.00 Noshes and snacks include dragon chips, tacos, zesty shrimp.

Drink Specials 2 $4.00 drafts; $3.00 wells; $1.00 off cocktails; Random specials like $2.00 Tuesdays

Atmosphere 3 Pass through the super-cute Tea Zone Café to discover a tucked-away speakeasy secret: the Camellia Lounge. Cozy, candlelit charm.

Cassidy's cassidysrestaurant.com

Downtown (West) Map
1331 SW Washington; (503) 223-0054

Happy Hours 4:00–6:00pm & 10:00–2:00am Daily

Food Deals 2 $5.75 Big, full-size servings of items like halibut corndogs, crab cakes, cheeseburger, salads, pizza, calamari, steamed mussels and prawns.

Drink Specials 0 Sadly, no drink specials

Atmosphere 2 Inside an old, historic building with lots of character following through inside (and it's perfectly positioned behind the Crystal Ballroom).

Clinton Corner Café

Southeast Map 2633 SE 21st Ave; (503) 230-8035
www.clintoncornercafe.net

Happy Hours 4:00–7:00pm Daily

Food Deals 2 $1.00 off menu items like sandwiches, salads, chips and dips.

Drink Specials 1 $.50 cents off beer, wine and mixed drinks/cocktails

Atmosphere 2
Cute, Mayberry-style café with slightly grittier bar side.

Crow Bar www.crowbarpdx.com

North/NE Map 3954 N Mississippi;(503) 280-7099

Happy Hours 3:00–8:00pm Daily (drinks)

Food Deals 2 $3.00–$4.00 Very limited but unique options like smoked salmon or hummus plates, Caesar salad.

Drink Specials 3 $3.00 microbrews; $1.50 PBR; $3.00 wines; $3.00 wells and martinis

Atmosphere 2 Dark basic bar with good tunes; low-key crowd of neighborhood hipsters plus random drop-ins. Rotating artist gallery.

Goodfoot www.thegoodfoot.com

Central Eastside 2845 SE Stark; (503) 239-9292

Happy Hours 5:00–9:00pm Mon–Fri (free pool too)

Food Deals 2 $5.00 Select menu items with semi-healthy pub food. Menu items under $7.00 at all times.

Drink Specials 2 $3.50 draft; $3.00 well drinks

Atmosphere 2
Big, open space showcases local artist rotating galleries and four red felt pool tables.

Hungry Tiger Too

Central Eastside Map 207 SE 12th; (503) 238-4321

Happy Hours 4:00–7:00pm Daily

Food Deals 2 $2.00–$5.00 Very vegan-friendly menu with lots of cheap eats.

Drink Specials 2 $1.00 off all beers and cocktails

Atmosphere 2 Wooden saloon bar with big tiger mural and café-like divebar-ish-ness, but not really.

Jade Lounge www.jadeloungepdx.com

Lloyd Center-ish 2342 SE Ankeny; (503) 236-4998

Happy Hours 5:00–7:00pm Daily
$3.00 Food Tuesday and Thursday all night★

Food Deals 2 $3.00–$5.00 Edamame, egg rolls,
seafood or veggie salad rolls, veggie tempura, satay.

Drink Specials 2 $1.00 off drafts & wine; $3.00
wells; $1.00 PBR and $2.00 microbrews all Sunday★

Atmosphere 2 Asian lounge with jade lanterns hung
from high ceilings and low coffee table seating.

Le Merde www.montageportland.com

Central East Side 301 SE Morrison; (503) 234-1324

Happy Hours 5:00–6:00pm Daily

Food Deals 2 $3.00–$4.00 Basics from Montage
next door: macaronis, gumbo, rice & beans, fritters
or maybe even gator bites!

Drink Specials 3 $3.00 draft beers, wine and wells

Atmosphere 1 Dark and different from sister
restaurant, Montage (which is kinda cute), Le Merde
is the lounge side (which is kinda grungy, but cool).

Leaky Roof www.theleakyroof.com

Downtown (off map)
1538 SW Jefferson St; (503) 222-3745

Happy Hours 3:30–6:00pm Mon–Fri

Food Deals 2 $2.50–$5.50 Tasty pub food varies
seasonally: Irish stew, burger, hummus plate, prawns.

Drink Specials 2 $1.00 off beer, wine & wells

Atmosphere 2 Very cozy Irish pub on a dark cold
night with open fireplace and wooden booths.

Liberty Glass

North/NE Map 938 N Cook; (503) 517-9931

Happy Hours 4:00–7:00pm and mid–2:30am Daily

Food Deals 0 $2.50–$13.00 Good menu, changes seasonally, but no discounts for Happy Hour.

Drink Specials 1 $1.00 off taps (early HH)

Atmosphere 2 Located in that cute pink house, they manned things up with antlers and woods. Has a peaceful 1776 Williamsburg cellar pub vibe.

Life of Riley

Pearl Map 300 NW 10th Ave.; (503) 224-1680

Happy Hours 4:00–7:00pm Daily

Food Deals 2 $2.50–$7.00 Tasty basics like buffalo wings, fries, kettle chips, sliders, grilled prawns.

Drink Specials 2 $2.00 domestics; $3.00 drafts (good tap list!), $1.00 off all drinks

Atmosphere 2 Large and open navy room; semi-retro, semi-Irish decor; rare ultra-casual option.

McFadden's www.mcfaddensportland.com

Old Town Map 107 NW Couch; (503) 220-5055

Happy Hours 4:00–7:00pm Mon–Sat

Food Deals 2 $2.00 Bar-style comfort food like chips and salsa, fries, mozzarella stix, quesadillas, hot wings, nachos, chicken tenders, and sliders.

Drink Specials 21 $2.00 Millers

Atmosphere 2 New look of old Irish Pub; big rooms with brick walls; huge party space with dance floor and many, many hi-def and flat screen TVs.

Muu-Muu's www.muumuus.net

612 NW 21st Ave.; (503) 223-8169

Happy Hours 3:00–7:00pm Daily

Food Deals 2 $2.00-$5.00 New 18-item menu goes all night! Spicy wings, beef and chicken satay, salad, calamari, hummus plate, steak bites, potstickers.

Drink Specials 3 $2.00 PBRs; $3.00 wells & micro-brews; $4.00 well martinis

Atmosphere 2 Chill, traveler's-style bar with black, tin ceiling tiles, orange hanging lights; velvet drapes, giant urn lamps, and tiny bubble lights.

New Old Lompoc

1616 NW 23rd; (503) 225-1855

Happy Hours 3:00–6:00pm & 10-close Mon–Fri
★Drink specials all day Sat and Sun
$2.50 drafts Mondays; $3.00 Bloody Marys Sunday

Food Deals 2 $2.00 off appetizers
Smaller menu with calamari, nachos, garlic dip, fries.

Drink Specials 2 $3.25 pints; $1.00 off liquor

Atmosphere 2 Heavenly hops-covered back patio is the biggest draw here. Laid-back casual scene with picnic tables both inside and out.

Nightlight Lounge

2100 SE Clinton; (503) 731-6500
www.nightlightlounge.net

Happy Hours 3:00–7:00pm Daily

Food Deals 2 $3.00–$5.00 Soup, salad, grilled cheese, Caesar salad, quesadilla, mac & cheese; nachos.

Drink Specials 2 $3.50 microbrews; $1.50 PBRs; $.50 off well drinks; $1.00 off wine

Atmosphere 2 Artsy, casual, and comfortable, yet trendy; outdoor dining on nice back deck.

Pala www.palalounge.com

Old Town Map 105 NW 3rd Ave.; (503) 242-0700

Happy Hours
9:00–10:30pm Thurs–Sat; 9:00–close Wednesday

Food Deals 2 $3.00 Mini-burgers, Cuban pork sandwiches, tater tots, fries, fried zucchini and mushrooms, pizza, ravioli, potstickers, calamari

Drink Specials 1 $3.00 well drinks

Atmosphere 2 Stark and simple underground brick tunnel effect with a touch of Indonesian flair thrown in.

Report Lounge

Central East Side 1101 E Burnside; (503) 236-6133

Happy Hours 4:00–7:00pm Mon–Sat

Food Deals 2 $3.00–$6.00 Bar standards like burger, wings, hummus, mac & cheese, nachos.

Drink Specials 1 Rotating nightly specials

Atmosphere 2 The old Chesterfield with toned-down murals, but ramped up edge. It's a club, not a pub. Windows open to sidewalk patio/eating area.

Rontoms www.rontoms.net

Central East Side 600 E Burnside (503) 236-4536

Happy Hours 4:30–6:30pm Daily

Food Deals 2 $4.00 Caesar, grilled cheese with soup, artichoke dip, tuna melt, and chicken sandwich.

Drink Specials 1 $1.00 off wells

Atmosphere 2
Big open room a la 1970s; giant party patio with ping pong; fireplace; lounge chair groupings.

Sagittarius

North/NE Map 2710 N Killingsworth; (503) 289-7557

Happy Hours 4:00–close Mon; 4:00-6:00pm Tues–Fri

Food Deals 2 $3.00–$5.00
Diner dinners with stylish home cookin'.

Drink Specials 2 $3.00 beer; $3.00 well drinks
$1.00 off wine and specialty cocktails

Atmosphere 2 Funky with coral walls and a groovy
60's vibe; hanging plastic bubble lamps, full mirrored
wall, and vintage astrology books.

Shanghai Tunnel Lounge

Old Town Map 211 SW Ankeny; (503) 220-4001
www.shanghaitunnel.com

Happy Hours 5:00–7:00pm Daily

Food Deals 3 $2.00–$4.00 Yummy pot stickers, quesadillas, nachos, veggie or chuck burgers, fries

Drink Specials 2 $1.00 off draft beers; $2.00 PBRs
$2.00 off wells

Atmosphere 2 Built over the underground Shanghai
tunnels; painted murals and simple Asian touches.

Slow Bar www.slowbar.net

North/NE Map 533 SE Grand; (503) 230-7767

Happy Hours 3:00–6:00pm Mon–Fri

Food Deals 2 $2.50–$5.50 Pizzetta, green salad,
mixed nuts, fries, ceviche, Southern fry, olives. Just
get the burger!

Drink Specials 2 $1.00 off beer; $2.50 well drinks

Atmosphere 2 Dark and smoky, laid-back popular
hipster scene; all black; group seating at window.

Someday Lounge

Old Town Map 125 NW 5th Ave; (503) 248-1030
www.somedaylounge.com

Happy Hours 4:00–8:00pm Mon–Fri

Food Deals 2 $2.00–$6.00 Healthy portions of
unique vegetarian fare including quesadillas, nachos
and sandwiches.

Drink Specials 3 $2.00 PBR; $1.50 off drafts, wells,
and specialty drinks; $4.00 wine

Atmosphere 2 An eclectic art and performance
space that's a touch rough around the edges.

Tiger's Cafe

SE Map 2045 SE Belmont; (503) 239-1887
www.tigerscafepdx.com

Happy Hours 4:00–7:00pm Mon–Sat

Food Deals 2 $3.00 appys, pizza, and sandwiches
(i.e. shawrama or falafel), hummus, baba ghannooj.

Drink Specials 2 $1.00 off cocktails ($3.00 wells)

Atmosphere 1 Big coffee counter at entrance with
Pepsi machine. It's a breakfast place with Lebonese
food and full bar, but closes at 7:00pm weekdays.

XV (15)

Old Town Map 15 SW 2nd Ave. (503) 790-9090
www.xvpdx.com

Happy Hours 4:00–7:00pm Daily

Food Deals 2 Half-off every food item on the menu
with big selection of good cheapies. $3.00 off pizzas.

Drink Specials 3
$1.50 off drafts ; $2.00 off wine, wells & cocktails

Atmosphere 2 Black and more black; regular bar
area, but cool restaurant and candle-lit lounge in
next room.

Cool Dive Bars

These are some fun places that are more casual than those in rest of book, but have style all their own. Cheap grub and drinks – and no smoking.

Ash Street Saloon
Old Town Map
225 SW Ash St; (503) 226-0430
www.ashstreetsaloon.com
<u>4:00–8:00pm Daily</u> $2.75 menu items
$1.25 PBRs; $2.75 micros & wells
Good sidewalk seating.

Bar of the Gods
Hawthorne Map
4801 SE Hawthorne; (503) 232-2037
<u>5:00–8:00pm Mon–Fri</u>
$1.00 PBRs; $2.50 wells
Great back patio.

Beulahland
Lloyd Center-ish Map
118 NE 28th Ave.; (503) 235-2794
<u>4:00–7:00pm Mon–Fri</u> $1.00 off menu items
$3.50 pints & $2.50 wells
Funky decked-out walls.

Captain Ankeny's
Old Town Map
50 SW 3rd Ave; (503) 223-1375
<u>4:00–7:00pm Daily</u> Rotating daily specials
$3.00 micros/imports; $3.00 wells
Good tap lineup.

Cool Dive Bars

Florida Room
North/NE Map
435 N. Killingsworth St. ; (503) 287-5658
<u>3:00–7:00pm Daily</u> $2.75 snacks
$.50 off cheap wells and taps
Budget beach decor. Known for weekend Bloody Marys.

Gypsy
Old Town Map
625 NW 21st Ave.; (503) 796-1859
<u>4:00–7:00pm Mon–Fri</u> $2.95–$4.95 big bar menu!
Rotating daily discounts; $1.00 off beers & wells
The Velvet Lounge in bar side is a bit more swanky.

Kelly's Olympian
Old Town Map
426 SW Washington; (503) 228-3669
<u>4:00–7:00pm Mon–Fri</u> $2.00–$4.00 menu
$3.00 well & micros
Motorcycles and garage stuff everywhere. Since 1902.

LaurelThirst Pub
Old Town Map
2958 NE Glisan; (503) 232-1504
<u>Before 5:00pm Mon–Fri</u> $3.50 micros
<u>6:00–8:00pm</u> Free live music
Sidewalk seating.

Lotus Room
Downtown (East) Map
932 SW Third Ave; (503) 227-6185
<u>3:00–7:00pm / 9:00pn–close Daily</u> $2.95–$4.95 apps
$3.00 wells & $3.50 drafts
Huge bar and cool back card room; sidewalk seating.

Low Brow Lounge

Old Town Map
1036 NW Hoyt; (503) 226-0200
<u>5:00–7:00pm Daily</u>
$1.00 off drafts; $3.00 wells
A famous favorite!

Matador

Old Town Map
1967 W Burnside St; (503) 222-5822
<u>Noon–7:00pm Daily</u>
$1.50 PBRs; $2.75 wells
Bull-fighting themed dive bar. Really.

Rogue Brewery

Pearl Map
1339 NW Flanders; (503) 222-5910 www.rogue.com
<u>3:00–5:00pm and 10:00pm–close Mon-Fri</u>
Discounted bar food, but sadly, no drink specials
Laid-back rogue-ish hangout; sidewalk seating.

Space Room

Southeast Map
4800 SE Hawthorne; (503) 235-8303
<u>11:00am–7:00pm Daily</u> $2.50 wells
Blacklight UFO theme.

Virginia Cafe

Downtown (West) Map
820 SW 10th Ave.; (503) 227-8617
<u>4:00–7:00pm Mon–Fri</u> Cheap bar-style eats
$2.50 domestics; $3.50 micros; Double-ups wells
*It s transplanted, new home retains just a bit of
the old, nostalgic charm. Now more caf -y.*

Beaverton
(Cedar Hills Mall Area)

Century 16 Movies

Bugatti's

Walker Rd.

Walker Rd.

Exit 1

McGrath's

Cedar Hills Blvd.

217

Hall Blvd.

Hall St. Grill

Mingo Typhoon

Exit 2A

SW Canyon Rd. (8)

Farmington

Decarli 1st

(10) Beaverton-Hillsdale Hwy

Watson

Hall

McCormick & Schmick's

Stockpot

1 mile

Bugatti's

● ● ● ● ● ● ● ● ● ● ● ● ● ● ● ● ● ●

8

Beaverton Map
2905 SW Cedar Hills Blvd.; (503) 626-1400
<u>Also in Beaverton</u>
Amber Glen (Tanasbourne)
2364 NW Amber Brook; (503) 352-5252
<u>West Linn (opens 4:30pm, no drink specials)</u>
18740 Willamette; (503) 636-9555
<u>Oregon City</u>
334 Warner Milne; (503) 722-8222
www.bugattisrestaurants.com

Happy Hours
3:00–6:00pm and 8:00pm–close Daily

Food Deals 3
$2.00–$5.00
New menu (slight varies per place): garlic prawns,
salads, tortellini, pizza, pasta, calamari, soup.

Drink Specials 2 $1.00 off beer, wine and wells

Atmosphere 2
Basic bar areas compared to the somewhat
fancier attached restaurants. All quite nice though
and more modern than old Italian in style.

Date visited: ....

Went with: ....

Notes: ....

....

....

My rating: ....

Decarli

4545 SW Watson Avenue
(503) 641-3223
www.decarlirestaurant.com

Happy Hours
4:30–6:00pm and 9:00pm–close Wed–Sat
★ All night Sunday (5:00–9:00pm)

Food Deals 3
$2.00–$7.00
Long list of half-off bar menu items! Good stuff like choice of several pizzas or paninis; burger with fries, salads, bruschetta, meatballs, fries.

Drink Specials 3
$3.00 draft beer: $5.00 house wines
$5.00 specialty cocktail

Atmosphere 3
Warm and welcoming with exposed red brick walls and an open kitchen. A neighborhood gem at home in the suburbs, but that seems more like a friendly, local New York hangout.

Date visited: _____

Went with: _____

Notes: _____

_____

_____

My rating: _____

Hall Street Grill

BEST OF BEAVERTON!

Beaverton Map
3775 SW Hall
(503) 641-6161
www.hallstreetgrill.com

Happy Hours
3:00–6:00pm and 9:00pm–close Mon–Sat
★ All night Sunday (4:00–10:00pm)

Food Deals 3
$2.95–$6.50
High-end restaurant = yummy Happy Hour eats!
Prime rib coyotas, coconut prawns, lettuce wraps,
burgers, steak bites, chicken salad sandwich,
hummus, fries, chips & dip, famous Caesar.

Drink Specials 3
$3.50 drafts; $4.50 wine; $4.25 sangrias
$4.00 wells; $4.00–$5.00 cocktails

Atmosphere 3
Big and bustling Happy Hour scene inside what
is arguably the nicest place in Beaverton. Pacific
Northwest stylings with lots of wood. Love it!

Date visited: _____

Went with: _____

Notes: _____

_____

_____

My rating: _____

McCormick&Schmick's

Beaverton Map
9945 SW Beaverton-Hillsdale Hwy.
(503) 643-1322
www.mccormickandschmicks.com

Happy Hours
3:00–6:00pm Mon–Sat; 4:00–6:00pm Sun
9:00–11:00pm Sun–Thur; 9:30pm–mid Fri-Sat

Food Deals 3
$1.95–$4.95
Over a dozen menu items at four price tiers
including a cheeseburger with fries for only $2.95!
Fish tacos, ravioli, quesadilla, clam strips, ahi tuna
roll, veggie nori roll, hummus plate, dip, mussels.

Drink Specials 1
Rotating nightly specials like $6.00 martinis

Atmosphere 3
Another superbly popular Happy Hour by my
heroes at M&S. Fun upscale dining and drinking
in upscale warehouse-style bar area.

Date visited: _____

Went with: _____

Notes: _____

_____

_____

My rating: _____

McGrath's Fish House

Beaverton Map
3211 SW Cedar Hills Blvd.; (503) 646-1881
<u>Milwaukee</u>
11050 SE Oak; (503) 653-8070
<u>Vancouver</u>
12501 SE Second Circle; (360) 514-9555
www.mcgrathsfishhouse.com

Happy Hours
3:00–6:00pm and 10:00pm–close Mon–Thurs
3:00–5:00pm Friday

Food Deals 3
$2.99
Unique spins on bar menu like salmon stack,
Asian ahi nachos, salad, pizza crackers, shrooms.

Drink Specials 3
$3.00/$4.00 tap beer; $3.50 wine
$3.50 wells; $4.50 select cocktails

Atmosphere 3
Casually-quaint waterfront fish house decor,
with nautical knick-knacks covering pretty much
every inch of space of their cavernous rooms.

Date visited: _____

Went with: _____

Notes: _____

_____

_____

My rating: _____

Mingo

. . . .

Beaverton Map
12600 SW Crescent (The Round)
(503) 646-6464
www.mingowest.com

Happy Hours
2:30–6:00pm Tues-Fri; 5:00–6:00pm Sun–Mon

Food Deals 2
$5.00–$7.00
Caprese, salad, shrimp skewers, pizzas,
burgers, penne pasta, bucatini, focaccia.

Drink Specials 3
$3.00 beer; $4.00 red or white wine
$5.00 wells; $6.00 daily cocktail

Atmosphere 3
Pea green walls, over-sized paper sculptures
and lanterns, and window-doors that open to an
inviting piazza with an outdoor Happy Hour bar.

Date visited: _____

Went with: _____

Notes: _____

_____

_____

My rating: _____

Stockpot Broiler

Beaverton (Not on Map)
8200 SW Scholls Ferry Rd.
(503) 643-5451
www.stockpot.ypguides.net

Happy Hours
4:00–6:00pm and 9:00pm–close Daily

Food Deals 3
$2.25–$3.95
Extensive menu of big, cheap servings includes
platter of giant onion rings, bruschetta, salad or
egg rolls, beef satay, nachos, brisket, burgers,
nuggets, and tots.

Drink Specials 2
$3.50 microbrews; $3.25 wells

Atmosphere 2
A dark lounge even by day with black tables
and chairs, bar rails, walls, bricks and fireplace.
Golf course views from wonderful seasonal
patio. Reminiscent of early 1980s decor with
music often reflecting that.

Date visited: _____

Went with: _____

Notes: _____

_____

_____

My rating: _____

Typhoon

12600 SW Crescent (The Round)
(503) 644-8010
www.typhoonrestaurants.com

Happy Hours
4:00–6:00pm Mon-Fri; 4:30–6:00pm Sun

Food Deals 3
$3.00–$5.00
The art of Thai cooking at Happy Hour prices:
papaya salad, pot stickers, spring rolls, pad thai,
prawns, tom kha soup, calamari, signature miang
kum (wraps), and much more.

Drink Specials 3
$3.00 beer; $4.00 house wine
$5.00 cocktail creation of the day

Atmosphere 3
Bamboo-extravaganza entrance with funky wood
fish hangings. Complete fortuitous Feng Shui
lineup of essential brick, glass, water and metal.

Date visited: _____

Went with: _____

Notes: _____

_____

_____

My rating: _____

Monteaux's Public House

Beaverton (Off Map) www.monteauxs.com
16165 SW Regatta Lane; (503) 439-9942

Happy Hours 3:00–6:00pm and 9:00pm–close Daily

Food Deals 2 $2.50–$5.00 Half-off appetizer menu of basic bar eats like quesadillas, nachos, hummus or "oomph" it with 20% off anything on dinner menu.

Drink Specials 2 $3.00-$4.00 beer; $3.00 wine or wells

Atmosphere 2 Turn-of-the-century charm mixed with modern-day neighborhood pub appeal, as depicted in their hand-painted mural.

Old Chicago

Beaverton (Off Map) www.oldchicago.com
17960 NW Evergreen Pkwy; (503) 533-4650

Happy Hours 3:00–6:00pm and 10:00pm–mid Daily

Food Deals 2 $2.99–$4.50 Big bar menu with nachos, salads, artichoke dip, pizza, wings.

Drink Specials 2 $3.29 micros & wells, $4.29 wine

Atmosphere 2 Sure it's a chain, but with 101 beers as a theme/tour, Chicago in the name, and 15 TVs.

Outback Steakhouse

Beaverton (Off Map) www.outback.com
11146 SW Barnes; (503) 643-8007

Happy Hours 4:00–6:00pm Mon–Fri

Food Deals 2 $3.50–$5.00 Meaty bar menu with items like cheeseburgers, pork sandwiches, shrooms, chopped steak & potatoes, quesadillas, mac & cheese.

Drink Specials 3 $2.00 domestics; $3.00 wine; $3.50 margaritas; $1.00 off cocktails

Atmosphere 2 Follows casually-fun, Outback-style.

Lake Oswego

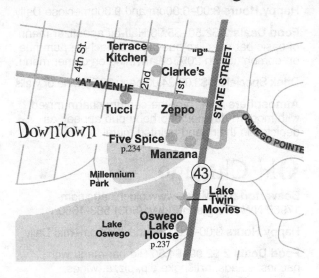

Terrace Kitchen

4th St.

2nd

"B"

Clarke's

"A" AVENUE

1st

STATE STREET

Tucci

Zeppo

OSWEGO POINTE

Downtown

Five Spice
p.234

Manzana

Millennium
Park

(43)

Lake
Twin
Movies

Lake
Oswego

Oswego
Lake
House
p.237

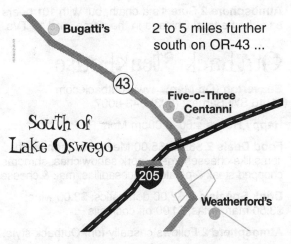

Bugatti's

2 to 5 miles further
south on OR-43 ...

(43)

Five-o-Three
Centanni

South of
Lake Oswego

205

Weatherford's

Centanni

Lake Oswego Map (South)
22000 Willamette Dr.; West Linn
(503) 722-9022
www.centannilounge.com

Happy Hours
4:00–6:00pm Daily

Food Deals 3
$4.00–$6.00
All you can eat pasta for only $6.00! I love the concept (your choice of five Italian classic dishes). Plus bruschetta, caprese or Caesar sides.

Drink Specials 3
$3.00 beer; $5.00 house wines; $5.00 martini

Atmosphere 3
Subdued, contemporary, city-style interior with clean lines and great attention to design details. Giant slide shows within frames showcase ever-changing photos and art. Located in a strip mall, but could work in New York.

Date visited: _____

Went with: _____

Notes: _____

_____

_____

My rating: _____

Clarke's

Downtown Map (Downtown)
455 2nd St.
(503) 636-2667
www.clarkesrestaurant.net

Happy Hours
4:30–6:00pm Mon–Sat

Food Deals 3
$1.00–$5.00
Half-off bar extra-delicious grub menu: quiche of the day, BBQ pulled pork quesadilla, burger, razor clams, croque monsieur, truffled fries.

Drink Specials 2
No corkage fee on Monday (added point for thinking of this concept!); 25% off wine bottles Wednesday.

Atmosphere 2
Tiny, but cozy & comfortable modern, bistro-style bar area. Nuetral tones with wine and bar as focal points. Outside summer patio seating.

Date visited: _____
Went with: _____
Notes: _____
_____
_____

My rating: _____

Five-o-Three

21900 Willamette Dr.; West Linn
(503) 607-0960
www.restaurant503.com

Happy Hours
3:00–6:00pm Mon–Fri

Food Deals 3
$4.00–$8.00
Soup and salad, pizza, burgers, BBQ chicken
or halibut sandwiches, mussels, mac & cheese,
pommes frites, artisan cheese plate.

Drink Specials 3
$3.00 drafts; $5.00 red or white wine or bubbly

Atmosphere 3
Warm tones with artistic flair looks coolest at
night! Big and welcoming front bar, but you are
welcome to sit anywhere in the restaurant at
Happy Hour. Pleasant and peaceful patio too.

Date visited: _____

Went with: _____

Notes: _____

_____

_____

My rating: _____

Manzana's

Lake Oswego Map (Downtown)
305 1st St.
(503) 675-3322
www.manzanagrill.com

Happy Hours
3:00–6:00pm and 9:00pm–close Daily

Food Deals 3
$2.00–$6.00
Chicken quesadilla, citrus honey chicken wings,
BBQ sandwich, hummus, Caesar, sliders, soup.

Drink Specials 3
$4.00 drafts; $4.00 red & white wine
$4.00 choice cocktails

Atmosphere 3
Mmmm... the rotisserie smell! Deep, dark, rich
wooden booths and walls (new and modern).
Big space attracts a crowd. Located right on the
lake, but Happy Hour seating inside only. Part
of the beloved Restaurants Unlimited Group.

Date visited: _____

Went with: _____

Notes: _____

_____

_____

My rating: _____

Terrace Kitchen

485 2nd St.
(503) 699-1136
www.terracekitchen.com

Happy Hours
5:00–6:00pm Tues–Sat

Food Deals 3
Five at $5.00
Superior quality in Happy Hour food! Artfully prepared and presented. As examples, items like hand-made tortilla chips (beautiful), veggie tempura, fish tacos, fritters, flat breads.

Drink Specials 1
$5.00 micros; $6.00–$7.00 choice wines

Atmosphere 3
Located in the building that formerly housed Amadeus Restaurant, remodel still retains historic look, though with a toned down and minimalist interior. Head for the outside terrace!

Date visited: _____

Went with: _____

Notes: _____

_____

_____

My rating: _____

Tucci

●●●●●●●●●●●●●●●●●●●●●●●

Lake Oswego Map (Downtown)
220 "A" Ave.
(503) 697-3383
www.tucci.biz

Happy Hours
4:00–6:00pm and 9:00pm–close Tues–Sat
★All night Monday; 4:00–6:00pm Sun

Food Deals 3
$5.00
Huge array of small plate "piadinas" includes
calamari, mussels, prawns, meatballs, various
bruschettas, pizzas, cheese or meat plates, plus!

Drink Specials 2
$4.00 draft beer; $5.00 red or white wine
$1.00 off wells and cocktails

Atmosphere 3
A very well-decorated, modernized old Italian-
style restaurant. Warm, golden tones, gorgeous
tile and iron work, rich dark woods and comfy,
upholstered seating.

Date visited: ....

Went with: ....

Notes: ....

....

....

My rating: ....

Weatherford's

Lake Oswego Map (South)
602 7th Street, Oregon City
(503) 723-9253
www.weatherfordsgrandlodge.com

Happy Hours
4:00–5:00pm Daily for the **$1.00 menu!**
5:00–6:30 Daily / 9:00-10:00pm Fri-Sat for $2 menu

Food Deals 3
$1.00–$2.00 menu
Yep – you read that right – 10 tasty treats for only
a buck each! Mini turkey wrap, beef kabobs, chix,
quesadilla, wings, egg roll, chips, shrimp salad.

Drink Specials 1
No specials, but $3-$4 beer and best cocktails!

Atmosphere 3
Housed inside a gorgeous, 1920s former Odd
Fellows Club mansion. Upscale, mellow and
very pleasant with buttercream walls, tin ceiling,
historic photos, and a 40 foot long bartop. Get
directions ahead of time as it's tricky traveling,
but worth a trip – take a joy ride down south!

Date visited: _____

Went with: _____

Notes: _____

_____

_____

My rating: _____

Zeppo

Lake Oswego Map (Downtown)
345 First St. Ste 105
503) 675-2726
www.zepporestaurant.com

Happy Hours
2:00–6:00pm and 8:00pm–close Daily

Food Deals 2
$4.50
Mixed-quality Italian eats like Margherita pizza,
Caesar and caprese salads, bruschetta, risotto
cakes w/red pepper, penne chicken & mushrooms, fettuccini, linguini, chicken skewers.

Drink Specials 2
$5.00 house wines; $5.00 cosmo

Atmosphere 3
Creative cutlery and kitchenware decor. Warm
and friendly place with central bar, copper-
topped tables and painted concrete floor. Cool
Leaning Tower of Pizza wall art.

Date visited: _____

Went with: _____

Notes: _____

_____

My rating: _____

Tigard Area

SW Pacific Hwy.

99

Exit 294

Newport Seafood

217

Exit 292

Oswego Grill

Kruse Way

Stanford's

SW 72nd Ave.

I-5

Carmen Dr.

Split

Sinju

Exit 290

Blue Tangerine

McCormick & Schmick's

P.F. Chang's

Claim Jumper

Player's

Hayden's and Bambuza

Exit 289

Blue Tangerine

Tigard Map
7361 SW Bridgeport Rd
(503) 620-9631
www.bluetangerinerestaurant.com

Happy Hours
3:00–6:00pm Mon–Fri

Food Deals 2
$3.00–$5.00
The price is right on Mediterranean favorites like hummus, chicken kabob sandwich, baba ganoush, eggplant dip, tabouleh, falafel sandwich, gyros, and pizza.

Drink Specials 1
$1.00 off beer and wine

Atmosphere 2
Casual café with lots of light via huge front windows; handpainted old-world map; nice Turkish touches. Magic point for decorating the high lofted ceiling with four giant curtain swags and a Moroccan hanging lantern.

Date visited:

Went with:

Notes:

My rating:

Claim Jumper

Tigard Map
18000 SW Lower Boones Ferry
(503) 670-1975
<u>Also in Clackamas Town Center</u>
9085 SE Sunnyside; (503) 654-3700
www.claimjumper.com

Happy Hours
3:00–7:00pm Mon–Fri

Food Deals 2
$2.00–$6.00
Big portions of tasty bar favorites including BBQ
mini-pizzas, nachos, wings, chicken tenders,
quesadillas, fish tacos and calamari.

Drink Specials 3
$3.25–$4.25 drafts; $4.00 wine and sangria
$2.00 off wells; $5.00 specialty drinks

Atmosphere 3
Inside and out it's rocks and big wooden timbers,
open air and ironworks. Experience the northwest
frontier from the comfort of your barstool.

Date visited: _____

Went with: _____

Notes: _____

_____

_____

My rating: _____

Hayden's

8187 SW Tualatin
(503) 885-9292
www.haydensgrill.com

Happy Hours
3:30–6:30pm and 9:00pm–close Daily

Food Deals 3
$3.95–$4.95
Bar classics plus better: super nachos with kettle chips, pepper bacon mac & cheese, teriyaki chicken bowl, beef tenders, salads, quesadilla, burgers, shrimp, wings, five spice pork shank.

Drink Specials 2
$1.00 off drafts and wells; $5.00 house wine

Atmosphere 3
Upscale and upbeat retro spin with color blocking and mod graphics. Good mix of private dining tables and more social cocktail area. Great stop when coming back from wine country!

Date visited: _____

Went with: _____

Notes: _____

_____

_____

My rating: _____

Oswego Grill

7 Centerpointe Dr.
(503) 352-4750
www.theoswegogrill.com

Happy Hours
3:00–6:00pm and 9:00pm–close Daily

Food Deals 3
$1.95–3.95
About a dozen bar basics: linguini, fries, fish tacos, artichoke dip, Caesar, pork sliders, soup.

Drink Specials 1
$1.00 off drafts

Atmosphere 2
It's the old Chili's off I-5, and almost a kind of new Stanford's in appearance, but not. Restaurant side is quite nice and traditional, but bar area for Happy Hour is a bit cramped and ordinary. Nice patio in the summer.

Date visited: _____

Went with: _____

Notes: _____

_____

_____

My rating: _____

Players

• •

7

Tigard Map (Lake Oswego)
17880 SW Lower Boones Ferry
(503) 726-GAME (4263)
www.eatdrinkbowlplay.com

Happy Hours
4:00–6:00pm Mon–Fri
8:00pm–close Mon–Thurs; All day Sunday★

Food Deals 2
$3.95
The full line-up of usual suspects in bar food:
sliders, fries, wings, nachos, quesadillas, pasta,
cheeseburger, Caesar salad, potato skins

Drink Specials 2
$2.50 domestics; $3.50 micro; $5.00 wells

Atmosphere 3
It's a high-concept family entertainment complex
with arcades and bowling, so if that's up your alley,
you'll love it. Tons of hi-def TVs, but may be hard
to hear above loud music and rowdy kids during
daytime. Fun party rooms and two bars.

Date visited: ....

Went with: ....

Notes: ....

....

....

My rating: ....

Sinju

BEST OF TIGARD!

7339 SW Bridgeport Rd
(503) 352-3815
www.sinjurestaurant.com

Happy Hours
3:00–6:00pm and 9:00pm–close Daily

Food Deals 3
$2.00–$6.00
15 options including a variety of rolls; gyoza, edamame, shrimp or veggie tempura, yakitori and their famous "heart attack."

Drink Specials 3
$3.00 beer; $6.00 wine; $6.00 sake
$4.00 wells; $7.00 specialty drinks

Atmosphere 3
Red! Fiery! I love it! This is the perfect place to come after a movie at Bridgeport. Great group room with red cast and open fireplace. Painted ceilings, wood-slat panels and grids bar it up.

Date visited: _____

Went with: _____

Notes: _____

_____

_____

My rating: _____

Split

7335 SW Bridgeport
(503) 639-5711
splitwinebar.com

Happy Hours
3:00–6:00pm and 9:00pm–close Daily

Food Deals 3
$2.95–4.95
Big, new menu with tasty bar-style selections:
fish tacos, gorgonzola cheese fries, sliders, zesty
hummus, cheese plate, calamari and soup.

Drink Specials 3
$1.00 off beer; $4.00 red or white wine
$3.50 wells, $5.00 cocktail of the day

Atmosphere 3
Meet a friend for a movie and hit Split before
or after the show and share in a mellow Happy
Hour. Neutral and contemporary decor takes
a cue from New York City bar *style*.

Date visited: _____

Went with: _____

Notes: _____

_____

_____

My rating: _____

See full listings in Portland section.

• •

McCormick & Schmick's

Tigard Map (Bridgeport Mall)
17015 SW 72nd Ave.; (503) 684-5490
www.mccormickandschmicks.com
3:00–6:00pm and 9:00pm–close Daily
Rotating daily drink specials. Food $1.95–$4.95

Newport Seafood Grill

Tigard Map
10935 SW 68th Pkwy; (503) 245-3474
www.newportseafoodgrill.com
3:00–7:00pm Daily; 9:00pm–close Daily
$3.00 beer, wine and wells! Food $3.00–$5.00

P.F. Changs

Tigard Map (Bridgeport Village)
7463 SW Bridgeport; (503) 430-3020
www.pfchangs.com
3:00–6:00pm Daily
$1.50 off beer, wine & cocktails, 1/2 off appetizers

Stanford's

Tigard Map (Lake Oswego)
14801 Kruse Oaks; (503) 620-3541
www.stanfords.com
3:00–6:00pm and 9:00pm–close Daily
All day/night Sundays
$3.50 beer, wine or wells! Food $1.95–$4.95

Vancouver

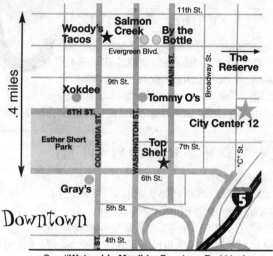

Woody's Tacos ★
Salmon Creek
By the Bottle

11th St.
Evergreen Blvd.
The Reserve

MAIN ST.
Broadway St.

9th St.

Xokdee
Tommy O's

8TH ST.
City Center 12 ★

Esther Short Park

7th St.
"C" St.

Top Shelf ★
6th St.

Gray's
5th St.

5

Downtown
4th St.

.4 miles

COLUMBIA ST.
WASHINGTON ST.

See **"Waterside Map"** for Beaches, Red Lion's
The Quay, McMennamin's, and Who Song & Larry's

Cactus Ya-Ya

MILL PLAIN
164th AVENUE

Far East

Gustav's
167th
18th
15th STREET

Big Al's
20th STREET

176th
192nd AVENUE
180th AVENUE

1.75 miles

VILLAGE LOOP

29th

162nd

Blackstone
34th STREET

164th AVENUE
CASCADE PKWY.

**Roo'
360**

Exit 8
Tommy O's

14
Exit 10

192nd AVENUE

Big Al's

Vancouver Map (Far East)
16615 SE 18th St
(360) 944-6118
www.ilovebigals.com

Happy Hours
3:00–6:00pm Mon–Fri;
9:00pm–close Mon–Thurs; 11:30pm–close Fri–Sat

Food Deals 2
$1.49–$3.99
Variety with the full array of bar eats, plus some
more interesting things like lasagna, gyros,
General Tsi's chicken, pita pizza, glazed riblets,
and brownies with ice cream.

Drink Specials 1
$2.00–$5.00 rotating specials on beer
and cocktails change weekly or so

Atmosphere 3
State-of-the-art bowling alley with stylish NW
lodge flair, flat screen monitors, bright lights and
loud noises. Cool back bowling party lounge!

Date visited: ....

Went with: ....

Notes: ....

....

....

My rating: ....

Blackstone

• • • • • • • • • • • • • • • • • •

Vancouver Map (Far East)
3200 SE 164th Ave
(360) 253-0253
www.blackstonewa.com

BEST OF VANCOUVER

Happy Hours
3:00–6:30pm and 9:00–11:00pm Mon–Sat
All day Sunday (2:30pm–close)★

Food Deals 3
$3.00–$5.00
Half-off incredibly extensive and stand-out bar
menu as in "WOW!" Over 25 items includes ahi,
BBQ ribs, salads, soup, goat cheese polenta,
wings, cheddar burger, mac & cheese, mud pie.

Drink Specials 3
$3.00–$4.00 Half-price! Mouth-watering array of
cocktails and martinis, plus beer & wine specials.

Atmosphere 3
A very popular and well-heeled scene. Upscale,
contemporary decor with walls of windows and low
tables. Weekend live music acts at Happy Hour.

Date visited: _____

Went with: _____

Notes: _____

_____

_____

My rating: _____

Cactus Ya-Ya

7

Vancouver Map (Far East)
15704 SE Mill Plain Blvd
(360) 944-9292

Happy Hours
3:00–6:00pm and 9:00pm–close Daily

Food Deals 3
$3.50
Super-delicious and famous ya-ya rolls (chicken, salmon or steak), nachos, fish taco, burger, quesadilla, skewers and salads.

Drink Specials 1
Rotating special of the day

Atmosphere 2
A happenin' and very popular area restaurant. Bar side thus gets packed, being somewhat small – locals just love it! Outdoor patio for overflow and fun. Artsy Mexicali touches with some cool ironworks, paintings, and sculptures.

Date visited: _____

Went with: _____

Notes: _____

_____

_____

My rating: _____

Gray's at the Park

Vancouver Map (Downtown)
301 W 6th St
(360) 828-4343
www.graysatthepark.com

Happy Hours
4:00–6:00pm Daily; 9:00–11:00pm Fri–Sat

Food Deals 3
$3.00–$5.00
Top restaurant quality at Happy Hour with items such as grilled sirloin brochette, cheddar burgers, crab cake, calamari, quesadilla, mussels, oysters.

Drink Specials 1
$1.00 off drafts

Atmosphere 3
Well, the Hilton's are just *fancy!* A gorgeous, sleek hotel lobby with contemporary style on through to the high-class, retro-mod lounge with fireplace.

Date visited: _____

Went with: _____

Notes: _____

_____

_____

My rating: _____

Lapellah

Waterfront Map
2520 Columbia House Blvd.
(360) 828-7911
www.lapellah.com

Happy Hours
3:30-6:00pm Daily plus 9:00–11:00pm Fri-Sat

Food Deals 2
$1.00–$6.00
Unique options with seasonal variations include
oysters rockefeller, salads, shrimp louie, calamari,
fish tacos, wild boar ribs, mac & cheese, burger

Drink Specials 3
$3.50 drafts; $4.00 wines; $4.00 sangria
$4.00 wells and $5.00 specialty cocktails

Atmosphere 3
Northwest-style, natural and woody interior is
much like that of their other upscale restaurant,
Roots. Central and long group table dominates
surrounding upolstered booths. Cool lighting.

Date visited: _____

Went with: _____

Notes: _____

_____

_____

My rating: _____

The Restaurant
at the Historic Reserve

Vancouver Map (off map)
1101 Officer's Row
(360) 906-1101
www.restauranthr.com

Happy Hours
4:00–6:00pm Wed–Fri

Food Deals 3
$4.00
Enjoy high-end restaurant quality food and
ambiance: Pot stickers, chicken quesadilla, fish
and chips, calamari, seasonal green salad, beef
skewers, Commander's burger.

Drink Specials 0
Sadly, no drink specials

Atmosphere 3
Inside the grounds of historic Fort Vancouver.
Charming, turn-of-the-century estate (Ulysses S.
Grant lived here in the 1850's). Worth a trip!

Date visited: _____

Went with: _____

Notes: _____

_____

_____

My rating: _____

Roots

. . . .

Vancouver Map (Far East)
19215 SE 34th St.; Camas
(360) 260-3001
www.rootsrestaurantandbar.com

Happy Hours
3:00–6:00pm Daily
9:00–11:00pm Fri–Sat

Food Deals 3
$3.00–$6.50
Fresh from the Northwest seasonal menu with items like cheese plates, penne, prawns, soups, wings, burger, and several salad alternatives.

Drink Specials 2
$3.50 draft beer; $5.00 red and white wines
$4.25 well drinks; $5.75 select cocktails

Atmosphere 3
Understated and dimly-lit bar in the Riverstone Marketplace. Pacific Northwest style inside and out. Neutral tones and lots of wood and slate.

Date visited: _____
Went with: _____
Notes: _____
_____
_____

My rating: _____

Tiger's Garden/Xokdee Lounge

8

312 W. 8th St.
(360) 693-9585

Happy Hours
4:00–6:00pm Mon–Sat; 4:00–9:00pm Sun★
9:00–11:00pm Mon–Thurs; 9:00pm–mid Fri–Sat

Food Deals 2
$3.00
Appetizers like egg rolls, salad rolls, fried tofu,
wontons, satay, wings, California rolls.

Drink Specials 2
$2.50 drafts; $3.50 wells

Atmosphere 3
Tiger's Garden Restaurant lounge. Lots of comfy,
cushy, couch seating. Artistic glass lamps hang
low over bar; swanky red brocade curtains hang
high over large windows.

Date visited: _____
Went with: _____
Notes: _____
_____
_____

My rating: _____

Tommy O's

Vancouver Map (Two locations)
801 Washington St.; (360) 694-5107
4101 Se 192nd Ave; (360) 892-2484
www.tommyosaloha.com

Happy Hours
3:00–6:00pm Daily; 9:00–11:00pm Fri–Sat

Food Deals 3
$3.00-$5.00
A dozen or so tropically-themed eats like fish cakes, skewers, wings, beef ribs, fries, coconut shrimp, salad, calamari, quesadilla, spring rolls.

Drink Specials 3
$1.00 off drafts; $4.50 red and white wine
$4.50 specialty cocktails like mai-tais

Atmosphere 3
Tommy Bahama refinement in this upscale Hawaiian lounge next door to Tommy's restaurant. Wicker lounge chairs, huge bar, natural tones, bamboo, and surfboards. Live music weekends downtown. East side bar is quite small and doesn't have quite as much of the full-on Hawaiian feel.

Date visited: ....

Went with: ....

Notes: ....

....

....

My rating: ....

Vinotopia

11700 Se 7th St.
(360) 213-2800
www.cinetopiatheater.com

Happy Hours
3:00–6:00pm and 8:00–10:00pm Daily

Food Deals 3
$3.99
Back to basics: chicken satay, fish & chips, bacon-wrapped shrimp, nachos supreme, pot pie, meatloaf burger, artichoke dip & chips.

Drink Specials 2
$2.99 Miller Lite; $3.99 microbrews; $4.99 wine (steward's choice)

Atmosphere 3
Inside Cinetopia movie theater. Big and open restaurant with stunning fireplace area to enjoy dining inside, or weather permitting, a serene outdoor garden patio with flowers and fountains.

Date visited: _____

Went with: _____

Notes: _____

_____

_____

My rating: _____

Woody's Tacos

9

Vancouver Map (Downtown)
210 W Evergreen Blvd.
(360) 718-8193
www.woodystacos.com

Happy Hours
4:00–7:00pm Mon-Sat

Food Deals 3
$1.00–$3.00
Surprisingly delicious Mexican food for cheap!
Chips & salsa, poppers, garnachas, mushroom
and goat cheese chalupas, skewers and ceviche.

Drink Specials 3
$2.50 and $3.00 beers; $4.00 wells
$5.00 margaritas and specials on giant microbrews

Atmosphere 2
Order at Woody's counter, then sit out in the
indoor piazza area where you'll be surrounded
by quaint shops, galleries and artwork. Quite
unique – quiet and sweet, especially at night.

Date visited: _____

Went with: _____

Notes: _____

_____

_____

My rating: _____

360° Pizzeria www.360pizzeria.com

Vancouver (East) 3425 SE 192nd; (360) 260-3605

Happy Hours 4:00–6:00pm Daily

Food Deals 2 $1.00–$3.00 off regular menu prices: Pizza slices; small plates like bruschetta, grilled pesto prawns or meatballs; many pastas and salads.

Drink Specials 3 $3.00 beer; $4.50 wine; $5.00 mixed

Atmosphere 2 RIght across the parking lot from sister restaurant, Roots. Colorful and cool with patio.

The Rock www.therockwfp.com

Waterfront Map
2420 Columbia House Blvd; (360) 695-7625

Happy Hours 3:00-6:00pm / 9:00-11:00pm Mon–Fri

Food Deals 2 $3.00–$7.00 Half-price appetizers plus personal pizzas, mini burgers and wings.

Drink Specials 3 $2.75 drafts, wine and wells; $2.00 off "buckets"

Atmosphere 2 Mini chain of Washington wood-fired pizza joints with very fun, casual, collegiate feel.

Top Shelf

Vancouver (Downtown) 600 Main; (360) 699-7106

Happy Hours 4:00–7:00pm Mon–Fri

Food Deals 2 $4.00–$6.00 Small-ish Happy Hour menu with Caesar salad, pork shanks, wings, fondue, spinach dip and a sampler sausage plate.

Drink Specials 2 $6.00 selected martinis and wells

Atmosphere 2 Big U-shaped, central copper-top bar and 18-foot brick walls; comfortable, Irish bar effect; not fancy like the Top Shelf name might imply.

✂ •

Happy Hour food prices all night

Get Happy Hour prices on food 'til close.

Good for whole table (limit 8 people). Expires 12/30/10.

Belly

• •

2-for-1 Entree

Buy one entree **belly**...get one free!

Buy any dinner entree and get a second one of equal or lesser value absolutely free. Expires Dec. 30, 2010. Not good with any other offer. One coupon per table.

Belly

• •

Happy Hour food prices all night

Get Happy Hour prices on food 'til close.

No coupon necessary. Offer good at all times when you sit at the bar top.

Mint/820
816 N Russell St
Portland, OR 97227
(503) 284-5518
www.mintand820.com

Belly
3500 NE MLK Jr Blvd
Portland, OR 97212
(503) 294-9764
www.bellyrestaurant.com

Belly
3500 NE MLK Jr Blvd
Portland, OR 97212
(503) 294-9764
www.bellyrestaurant.com

Blitz Pearl

2-for-1 Any Menu Item

Buy any sandwich, salad or burger and get a second one of equal or lesser value absolutely free. Expires Dec. 30, 2010. Not good with any other offer. Limit one free item per table.

Blitz Ladd

2-for-1 Entree

Buy one entree ...get one free!

Buy any dinner entree and get a second one of equal or lesser value absolutely free. Excludes pizzas. Expires Dec. 30, 2010. Not good with any other offer. One coupon per table.

Gotham Tavern

Happy Hour food prices all night

Get Happy Hour prices on food 'til close.
Good for up to 20 people (must RSVP). Expires 12/30/10.

Blitz Pearl
110 NW 10th Street
Portland, OR 97206
(503) 222-2229
www.blitzpdx.com

Blitz Ladd
2239 SE 11th Ave
Portland, OR 97214
(503) 236-3592
www.blitzpdx.com

Gotham Tavern
2240 N Interstate Ave
Portland, OR 97227
(503) 517-9911
www.gothamtavern.com

Macadam's

2-for-1 Dinner Entree

Buy one entree and get one free!

Buy any dinner entree and get a second one of equal or lesser value absolutely free. Not good with any other offer. One coupon per table. Not redeemable for cash. Expires 12/30/10.

Melt

2-for-1 Sandwich

Buy one sandwich – get one free!

Buy any full size sandwich and get a second one of equal or lesser value absolutely free. Not good with any other offer. One coupon per table. Expires 12/30/10.

Oba!

2-for-1 Dinner Entree

Buy one entree  ...get one free!

Buy any dinner entree and get a second one of equal or lesser value absolutely free. Expires Dec. 30, 2010. Not good with any other offer. One coupon per table.

Macadam's
5833 SW Macadam Avenue
Portland, Oregon 97239
(503) 503.246.MACS
www.macadamsbarandgrill.com

Melt
716 NW 21st Ave.
Portland, OR 97209
(503) 295-4944
www.meltportland.com

Oba!
555 NW 12th Ave
Portland, OR 97209
(503) 228-6161
www.obarestaurant.com

North 45

Happy Hour food prices all night

Get Happy Hour prices on food 'til close.

Valid Sunday-Thursday only. Expires 12/30/10.

Paddy's

Happy Hour food prices all night

Get Happy Hour prices on food 'til close.

Valid Sunday-Thursday only. Expires 12/30/10.

Salty's

Free Entree

Buy one entree ...get one free!

Buy any dinner entree and get a second one of equal or lesser value absolutely free. Expires Dec. 30, 2010. Not good with any other offer. One per table. Portland/Columbia location only.

North 45
517 NW 21st Avenue
Portland, OR 97209
(503) 248-6317
www.north45pub.com

Paddy's
65 SW Yamhill St
Portland, OR 97204
(503) 224-5626
www.paddys.com

Salty's
3839 NE Marine Dr
Portland, OR 97211
(503) 288-3426
www.saltys.com

Tapalaya

✂ ┄┄┄┄┄┄┄┄┄┄┄┄┄┄┄┄┄┄┄┄┄┄┄

Happy Hour food prices all night

TAPALAYA

Get Happy Hour prices on food 'til close.

Valid Sunday-Thursday only. Expires 12/30/10.

Thirst Wine Bar & Bistro

2-for-1 Entree

Buy one entree  ...get one free!

Buy any entree priced at $17.00 or less and get a second one of equal or lesser value absolutely free. May not be used on holidays or with any other promotion or discount. One per table. Expires Dec. 30, 2010.

Wild Abandon

2-for-1 Entree

Wild Abandon

Buy one entree (dinner or breakfast/lunch),
get another of equal or lesser value free.

Not Valid Saturday or Sunday breakfast/lunch. Not valid on New Years Eve, Valentines Day or April 21st 14th Anniversary Party. One coupon per table. Expires 12/30/10.

Tapalaya
28 NE 28th Ave
Portland, OR 97232
(503) 232-6652
www.tapalaya.com

Thirst Wine Bar & Bistro
315 SW Montgomery St
Portland, OR 97201
(503) 295-2747
www.thirstwinebar.com

Wild Abandon
2411 SE Belmont St
Portland, OR 97214
(503) 232-4458
www.wildabandonrestaurant.com

Like deals?

Coupons are the new cool!

The Happy Hour Guidebook is excited to announce partnership with a new "mobile coupons" cell phone app called **mobons**! Now available on iPhones and iTouch, with expanded platforms coming soon, it's a great new way to find great new deals at your fingertips.

www.mobons.com

• • • • • • • • • • • • • • • •

Look for window stickers outside area restaurants – You can be sure there's a great Happy Hour and a refreshing drink waiting for you inside! This "stamp of approval" also codes exceptional Happy Hour places via mobons.

Notes

About the Author

Cindy Anderson created the Happy Hour Guidebook series in 2006. This is the fourth edition. She came up with the idea by realizing that Happy Hour hunting was hard to figure out! She developed a system of objectively rating Happy Hours (with a focus on nice restaurants rather than bars), and comparing their food deals, drink specials, and overall ambiance. The book format makes it easy to reference information quickly, and in relation to other Happy Hours. The plotted maps are easy to read, information is bullet-pointed and easy to find, ratings stand out clearly – and there's great coupons!

Originally from Chicago, Cindy loves Happy Hours and the pursuit of happiness, traveling, hiking, skiing, party buses, Jimmy Buffett, Elvis, naps, golfing, reading, painting, and all things Tiki. She also enjoys road-tripping, pub crawling and gallery hopping; mojitos, Margaritas and microbrews; imports, good wine, and just about everything that involves meeting up with a friend or two and having fun!

© 2009 Christina Weber

Twitter: PDXHappyHour

Become a fan on Facebook
Happy Hour Guidebook

Check website for maps and updates!
www.happyhourguidebook.com